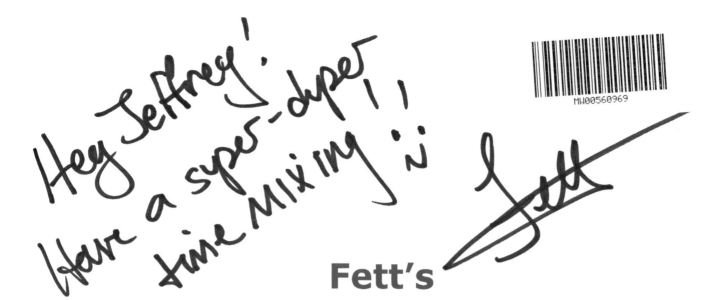

Hey Jeffrey! Have a super-duper time MIXING!! :^) —Fett

Fett's
Mixing Roadmap

A Step-by-Step Guide
To Mixing Music In The Studio

Azalea Music Publications
Nashville, TN

www.AzaleaMusic.com

MW00560969

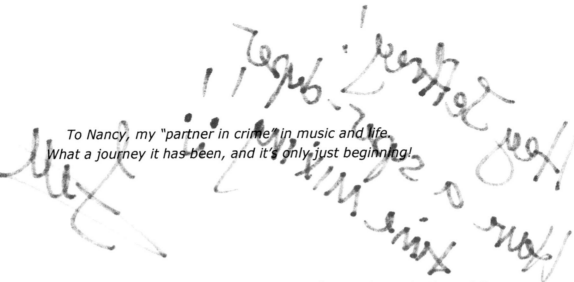

To Nancy, my "partner in crime" in music and life.
What a journey it has been, and it's only just beginning!

For more info on Fett and other educational resources for music production, visit:
www.AzaleaMusic.com

Disclaimer

This book is designed to provide information on music production. It is sold with the understanding that the publisher and author are not engaged in rendering legal, accounting, or other professional services. If legal or other expert assistance is required, the services of a competent professional should be sought.

It is not the purpose of this book to cover the full range of information that is otherwise available on this topic, but instead to complement, amplify, and supplement other texts. You are urged to read all available material and tailor the information to your individual needs.

Every effort has been made to make this book as accurate as possible. However, there may be mistakes, and with all the rapid changes online in particular, some details may be inaccurate by the time you read this. Therefore, this text should be used only as a general guide and not as the ultimate source of information on the topic.

The author and publisher shall have neither liability nor responsibility to any person or entity with respect to any loss or damage cause, or alleged to have been caused, directly or indirectly, by the information contained in this book.

Contents

INTRODUCTION 1

WHY THIS BOOK CAME ABOUT 1

A MIXING PHILOSOPHY 2

CHOOSING A MIXING PLATFORM 3

    Mixing "in the box" vs. "outside the box" 3

    Which computer-based mixing platform is right for you? 4

    Don't over-spend! 5

    A word about stealing: don't do it! 6

THE 7 PHASES OF THE MIXING PROCESS 7

MOMMY, HOW LONG DOES A MIX TAKE? 7

    Use and re-use 8

PHASE 1: ENVIRONMENT SETUP 10

DATA ORGANIZATION AND CONSISTENCY 10

    Naming consistency 10

    Drive and folder structure 10

        Project drive/Client Files folder 11

        DAW projects folders 14

        Song folders 14

        DAW-owned folders 15

        Imported Files folder 16

        Files To Be Sent folder 16

        Mixes, Etc folder 17

        Processed Files folder 18

        Encoded Files folder 19

        What about client- or song-specific presets? 19

PHASE 2: MIX SETUP AND MAINTENANCE 22

CREATE PROJECT (OR USE EXISTING ONE) 22

    Save and back up as you go! 22

IMPORT FILES TO TRACKS (OR USE EXISTING ONES) 24

GROUP TRACKS BY INSTRUMENTAL AND VOCAL "PARTS" 26

    Stereo vs. mono groups 26

ADD COLORS TO TRACKS/PARTS 28

TRIM SPACE FROM/CLEAN UP TRACKS 30

COMP TRACKS 33

PITCH-ADJUST TRACKS 35

CUT DOWN ON CLUTTER: PUT ASIDE UNUSED STUFF 37

INITIALIZE, SET ALL TRACKS TO NOMINAL LEVEL 37

ASSIGN INITIAL VIRTUAL INSTRUMENTS 40

CREATE INITIAL TIME-BASED EFFECTS 41

NEWS FLASH! PRESETS ARE YOUR BEST FRIEND 42

TAKE A BREAK, CHANGE HEADSPACE 44

PHASE 3: CORE MIX (VIRTUAL SOUND STAGE) **46**

Do "FULL UP AND DRY" LISTEN 46

THE 5 PRIMARY MIXING TOOLS 47

SET INITIAL RELATIVE LEVELS 47

    Initial drum levels and groups 50

SET INITIAL PANNING 51

    Drum orientation 52

    Listen in context and adjust 53

WHAT PART(S) TO START WITH? 54

ASSIGN INITIAL TIME-BASED INSERT/SEND EFFECTS 55

    How to set initial reverb levels 57

    Reverbs and front-to-back positioning 57

SET INITIAL EQ 59

    Finding the "tonal essence" of a part 60

    Additive vs. subtractive EQ 60

    EQ sweeping 63

    EQ spreading/splitting 66

    EQ flipping/swapping 66

    Listen in context and adjust 68

SET INITIAL COMPRESSION 68

    Compression threshold 69

    Compression ratio 72

    Compression attack and release 72

    Other aspects of compression 73

    Listen in context and adjust 74

CREATE AND ASSIGN EFFECTS FOR SPECIFIC PARTS 74

    Insert effects vs. send effects 75

        When to use insert vs. send 76

    Matching effects to their parts' stereo locations 78

SET INITIAL AUTOMATION FOR BASIC CONTROL 79

TAKE A BREAK, CHANGE HEADSPACE 80

PHASE 4: ITERATIVE ADJUSTMENT AND AUTOMATION **81**

RE-BALANCE PARTS 81

RE-CONSIDER ARRANGEMENT AND FLOW (AND ADJUST ACCORDINGLY) 81

    When a part participates (or not) 82

    The tone of a part 83

    Positioning a part 84

WHEN TO SAY "CHUCK IT!" 85

TAKE A BREAK, CHANGE HEADSPACE 86

PHASE 5: MASTER BUS PROCESSING AND TWEAKS **87**

MASTER BUS PROCESSING VS. MASTERING 88

DON'T TOUCH THAT DIAL! 88

Proper listening levels 89
    Crank it down! 89
Please leave the room... 90
Master bus mixing approaches 90
Master bus processors 91
Check/adjust master bus level 92
Set initial master bus EQ 95
Set initial master bus compression/limiting 96
    Compression, limiting, or both? 97
EQ, compression, or both? 98
Multi-band compression: combination EQ + compression in one step 98
Set initial master bus other effects 101
Retroactively adjust individual tracks/groups based on master bus changes 102
Re-check/adjust master bus level 102
Export mix to stereo file(s) 103
    Avoid MP3s at this stage 104
    Tracks-only mix 105
Take a break, change headspace 105

PHASE 6: MULTI-ENVIRONMENT LISTENING AND FINAL TWEAKS 106

Listen to exported mix in different environments...106
    The car test 106
    No changes yet, just listen... 106
    Speakers first, then headphones and ear buds 107
Make final adjustments to individual tracks, groups and master bus 107
When is a mix "finished?" 107
Re-export final mix to stereo file(s) 109

PHASE 7: WRAP-UP AND HOUSEKEEPING 111

After the mix is done: backups and archives 111
    Backup media options 111
    One for me, one for you... 111
    Remote backups 112
    Pie in the sky 112
    Archival storage 112
Celebrate! 113

Introduction

Why this book came about

I've been in the music recording business for more than thirty years. And for more than twenty of those years, I've done a lot of training, consulting, mentoring and coaching for home and project studio enthusiasts, as well as up-and-coming professional producers and engineers. Often, my clients already possess many of the elements it takes to do a great job at producing, recording and mixing, but in many cases, one thing they lack is a *system* – a process, methodology, or framework – for how they do they do their work. Their work habits just sort of evolve willy-nilly as needs arise, and as they become more familiar with their gear and the music production process. The end result is often messy and complicated, and in the extreme, even gets in the way of creating, recording and producing music – and the joy that's supposed to come with it.

One of the reasons for this haphazard development of production habits is that, unlike a few decades ago, there is no longer a mentoring process in the recording studio world. Back in the day, large, commercial studios would hire interns who would absorb excellent habits, tricks and secrets from seasoned pros. With the advent of home and project studios, and the consequent demise of most of the world's classical-model professional facilities, there's no longer a place to learn those day-to-day habits except by seat of the pants. I was lucky enough to be around for a little of the old-school model, but I, like many of my clients, learned a lot of stuff the hard way, through trial and error (and the occasional disaster) along the way. Over time, as my production career evolved from recording my own and my friends' music to taking on real, honest-to-goodness production clients, I was forced to develop a system of habits and practices – if for no other reason than to keep up with the sheer volume of projects that accumulated over the years.

After many years (and a lot of scars!), I've developed a fairly clean and methodical approach to the entire music production process, from initial client meetings to handing over a final master. A huge part of that process is, of course, mixing. It can be a very complex and tedious – even overwhelming – process, or it can be a joyous time when the fruits of all our creative efforts come together. Having a system and a methodology – from organizing and naming things usefully, to listening to and adjusting things in the right order – can to a lot to make the experience more of the joyful kind.

So, here's a book about the *process* of mixing. It's not a book about every possible tweak you could ever make to a kick drum track or the mechanics of operating any particular DAW – there are tons of books and other resources available that address all that stuff, and address it well. And while I do talk specifics and divulge many pro mixing secrets in the course of this book, the focus is primarily on keeping things streamlined and methodical.

A mixing philosophy

Before we go any further, it's important to explain that my approach to mixing is based on two fundamental tenets:

- The overriding goal of mixing is to most effectively convey the message and the feeling of the song for the purpose at hand; and
- *There are no rules* in mixing, only guidelines.

Note that I clarify the overriding goal above with "for the purpose at hand." One of the biggest mistakes I see inexperienced mixers make is to assume that a song or a project can be mixed the same way regardless of how the mixes will end up being used. Nothing could be further from the truth! Before you ever start mixing a song, you need to be very clear on *why* you are mixing it in the first place, and *who* will be the primary end listener(s). For example:

- Will the mix be used as part of collection of songs on an artist's commercial CD release?
- Will it be used for publishing pitches, for other artists to potentially record the song?
- Will it be released exclusively for digital download?
- Will it be used as part of the soundtrack for a film or a TV show?
- Is it just for posterity, or to capture ideas faithfully?
- Will it be used for a combination of purposes, implying that some compromises might need to be made?

Whenever I mix a song or a project for a client, I ask of a lot of questions like these up front. And the answers I get will have a huge impact on the overall approach I take, and the many decisions I make along the way. So get crystal-clear on the *purpose* of your mixes and the intended audience – before you start mixing!

Keep in mind that this is just one person's approach, based on decades of personal experience. It's not the only way to approach the mixing process, and not necessarily the "best way" for everyone or every situation. But after doing a couple thousand mixes on a variety of platforms over the years, I'm confident that it's a way that, when actually applied, works extremely well.

Choosing a mixing platform

Before we dive in, let's talk a little about what kind of equipment we'll actually be mixing on.

Mixing "in the box" vs. "outside the box"

There are two primary (and very different) methods for mixing music nowadays: "in the box" and "outside the box." In this context, "the box" is a computer. More traditional, "outside the box" mixing is done on a conventional hardware console (very often an analog one) and takes advantage of the console's physical layout and sonic characteristics through on-board faders and knobs, channel effects like compression/limiting, EQ (equalization), etc., bussing architecture, and signal routing capabilities. More often than not, "outside the box" mixing also takes advantage of other external (again, often analog) hardware devices like classic compressor/limiters, EQs (equalizers), effects units (such as reverbs, delays, etc.) and even preamps. Major benefits of console-based mixing include its tactile operation and sonic quality. But it's also generally very labor-intensive, time-consuming and expensive. It also doesn't lend itself well to replicability; re-setting up a traditional analog console for even a simple mix tweak can be a daunting task, and there's no guarantee that any unchanged parts will sound *exactly* the same each time.

Arguments rage as to which method of mixing (or a hybrid) is "better," but the bottom line is that, for all but a very privileged few at the top, most of today's mixes (including those from top-end professional facilities) are done "in the box," even if some external hardware is employed in the process. It's getting harder and harder to justify the effort and cost of mixing the "old-fashioned" way, but there's more to it than that. Most significantly, with "in the box" mixing, you have something that's simply impossible in the console-based world: potentially infinite numbers of tracks/channels, effects, and virtual instruments, limited only by the computer's processing power. If your computer can handle it, you can have 50 software-based Fairchild compressors running on a single mix, whereas a single "real" analog Fairchild (if you could even get your hands on one) would cost many, many thousands of dollars. Want to add another 30 tracks to the mix? There's need to worry about running out of channels. And you're guaranteed that if you run a mix 50 times in a row, it's going to sound *exactly* the same every time, no matter how complex it is.

For these reasons, this book assumes that readers are mixing "in the box." But keep in mind that the concepts and methodology presented here apply *regardless of your mixing platform*; I simply center the discussion and examples around the computer-based model and don't discuss differences between computer-based and console-based mixing. Even if I don't say it explicitly, for all of you (lucky!) console-based mixologists, the information is for you, too!

Which computer-based mixing platform is right for you?

Question #1: Mac or PC?
Answer: YES!

Question #2: Pro Tools, Cubase or Logic?
Answer: YES!

This is one of the areas of the audio production culture that I find absolutely hilarious. For so many years, I've heard many people (most of them painfully unqualified) arguing the merits of their particular combination of computer hardware, operating system and DAW (Digital Audio Workstation) software, while claiming that all others are *inferior*. Pro Tools on a Mac! SONAR on a PC! Audacity on Linux! Digital Performer or death! For these people, it's practically *religion*. I've even heard people say that Macs actually *sound* better than PC's, and vice-versa! Having spent the first twenty years of my music career also working in the computer industry, I can guarantee you that neither Macs nor PCs sound better or make better recordings. The software is another story, but even there, most of today's DAW software is not just great, but super-great. They're ALL good. Truth is, you can make ANY choice of platform work for you, and work extremely well. I've heard phenomenal-sounding recordings made with just GarageBand on an old, beat-up MacBook, and really, really awful-sounding recordings made with the most expensive, high-end Pro Tools HD system running on proprietary hardware. I've also heard so-called "lo-fi," 16-bit, 44.1 kHz recordings that sound fuller and have far more musical "depth" and "space" than 32-bit, 192 kHz ones. Trust me: the production skills you use are a thousand times more important than the hardware and software on which you apply them.

So what do I recommend? If you've bought this book about mixing, chances are you've already got a computer for music and are using some kind of recording software. My advice is, if you like what you've already got and it will also allow you to do mixing in addition to recording, then stick with what you have; it will do just fine. If you're not happy with the recording software you already have, or it's too limited for mixing, or you want to learn something new on purpose, then talk with your friends, read some online reviews, download some trial versions (many music software manufacturers offer them nowadays) and try them out. Then settle on whichever one feels the most comfortable and intuitive to you (remember, you're going to spend countless hours mixing with it, so it absolutely *has* to feel good), and it will serve you well.

Many DAW programs, such as Cakewalk SONAR, Adobe Audition, or Acoustica Mixcraft, run only on Windows; others, like MOTU Digital Performer and Apple Logic and GarageBand, run only on Macs. So, if compatibility with other studios and/or collaborators is important to you, you might want to go with something that's cross-platform (i.e., runs on both PCs and Macs) such as AVID Pro Tools, Cockos Reaper, PreSonus Studio One, or Steinberg Cubase and Nuendo.

On the hardware side, my first recommendation is to simply stick with whatever hardware and operating system you've already got, since you're already familiar with it. But if you're looking to upgrade your hardware because it might be running out of steam and doesn't have enough power to run many mixing plug-ins at a time, or you really don't like your current hardware and/or operating system, then I would recommend asking a trusted friend or two for advice. If they start getting all religious on you about how their computer brand or operating system *sounds* better than any other, or that all other computers or operating systems are pieces of junk or not "worthy of audio," then run the other way and find someone more objective to talk to. Right now, I have both Macs and PCs (and both desktops and laptops) in my studio, and they all work just fine for their defined purposes. I've also worked extensively on Unix-based systems in the past, and they rocked as well (although, in all fairness, your software options won't be as extensive for Unix-based platforms). My current "main" music production computer in my control room happens to be a custom-built PC, so all of the screenshots in this book came from that machine, but it just as easily could have been a Mac. It all comes down to this: ANY *properly-equipped and configured, reasonably current* computer can function perfectly well as a music mixing platform today.

Here's another way to look at it: at the end of the day, the end-listener of your music has *absolutely no idea* what computer, operating system, DAW program, software plug-ins – or any other gear, for that matter – you used to record and mix your music. All they care about is whether it *sounds good* to them and makes them *feel good*. When was the last time you heard someone say, "Damn, that song sounds great! I can tell it was recorded with a Neumann U87 mic through an M-Audio Octane preamp into an RME Hammerfall interface to Pro Tools running on a Dell tower under Windows 7, Service Pack 2!" What they do respond to is the quality of the song, the performance, and your recording, mixing and mastering chops. So keep your eye on the ball and make sure you don't get too hung up on all those other things that really don't matter in the long run. 'Nuff said!

Don't over-spend!

One non-platform-specific piece of advice I can give is, especially if you're just getting going, don't over-spend on your computer hardware and audio software. One of the biggest mistakes I see among both amateur and professional audio enthusiasts is the "sledgehammer-to-hit-a-thumbtack" approach: they buy much, much more capability than they need for the task at hand. Spending the most money you can does not necessarily translate to buying the best system for your purpose, level, or needs. If you're new to mixing, you don't have to buy a Super-Mac running Pro Tools HD or Nuendo and a UAD Quad card with a zillion whiz-bang plug-ins when a Gateway PC running native Pro Tools or Cubase with some native plug-ins will do the job more than adequately for a quite a while. As yours skills and needs increase, you can add on a bit at a time and work your way up gradually, and save a lot of money in the process.

Especially with computer hardware, capabilities skyrocket and prices plummet so fast that you're guaranteed to waste a lot of money if you buy the very top-of-the-line computer in terms of sheer power (processor speed, number of processor cores, speed and amount of memory, speed of data buses, etc.). Six months from now, you'll find the same thing for a lot less money, while something much less powerful (and costly) might have done the job just fine in the meantime. A computer with currently mid-level to upper-mid-level specs will do surprisingly well for most people as an audio mixing computer – as long as it is *properly set up and configured*. I can't stress enough that the right setup and configuration of your hardware and operating system can actually get you much more juice than a computer with simply higher "specs." Spend some of the money you save on the services of a good audio-computer consultant; it's a much better investment, and you'll gain a lot of valuable insight in the process. You can always add more memory, peripherals and hard drive space – even upgrade the CPU – a bit at a time as needed, and end up spending less money in the long run.

Similarly, in the software realm, I strongly recommend that people start with the lowest-level version of DAW software that they need, and upgrade to higher-level versions over time. For some bizarre reason, the "LE" versions of DAW programs are pooh-pooh'd by a lot of folks as somehow being of inferior quality to their higher-level cousins. Most of the time, the underlying audio engine is exactly the same, and the only differences are feature- or quantity-based – e.g., you may be limited in the number of tracks or simultaneous insert/send effects, or have less "stock" virtual instrument plug-ins – but so what if the LE version provides everything you need? Often, audio/MIDI interface manufacturers will bundle their hardware with free LE versions of popular software (Cubase, SONAR, etc.) as well as LE or trial versions of software plug-ins and other cool audio tools. Don't dismiss these add-on, packaged versions; they may be all you need for now. For example, you can start with Cubase LE, then upgrade to Cubase Artist, then upgrade to full-blown Cubase over time, and with upgrade pricing specials that run from time to time, end up spending less in total than you would have for the full-blown version of Cubase in the first place.

A word about stealing: don't do it!

If you haven't guessed already, I'm quite a pragmatist when it comes to audio production tools. ☺ I'm also a stickler (some would say a fanatic) when it comes to pirated software. The bottom line: there is absolutely NO justification for it. If you acquire and use "cracked" versions of software by whatever means, you are committing *theft*, plain and simple. Just because you can do it, it doesn't make it justifiable. It baffles me when people who produce *music* of all things can somehow rationalize stealing someone else's intellectual property. Imagine if you had to do all of your music writing, performing, recording and mixing for free, and never have your fans or clients pay you for any of it. That's what you're doing when you use an illegal copy of a company's software.

Beyond the ethical reasons for not stealing software, I look at it from a *value* point of view: for a few hundred bucks at most, you can have capabilities at your fingertips that you could only dream of – and would have cost tens of thousands of dollars or more in equivalent hardware – just a few years ago. Looking at it this way, music production software is *phenomenally inexpensive* for what you get. If we can justify paying a couple grand for a nice Taylor or Martin acoustic guitar (and there's definitely nothing wrong with that!), then we can certainly find a way to pay a couple hundred bucks for phenomenally feature-rich DAW software or twenty bucks for a cool compressor plug-in. If we want the amazing people who work for today's music software companies to continue to be able to bring us all of the wonderful capabilities that they do, then we have to keep them employed. And that means paying them for the products we use. Hope I've made myself clear about this...! ☺

The 7 phases of the mixing process

So let's get started. I see the mixing process as a series of very distinct *phases*, each with its own purpose, and just as important, its own *mindset*. Nothing will kill the creative process more than having to switch, in the middle of mixing a song, from a totally creative, right-brained activity (like getting the right "*pop!*" out of a snare drum), to something totally mechanical and left-brained (like finding the right noise-reduction plug-in to clean up a noisy guitar track). As a result, I try as much as possible to separate the left- and right-brained activities into separate phases. I also strongly recommend taking breaks between the different phases – both to give your ears a much-needed rest, and to give your brain a chance to "switch gears" between the different mindsets required for each phase. Here are the phases:

1. Environment Setup
2. Mix Setup and Maintenance
3. Core Mix (The Virtual Sound Stage)
4. Iterative Adjustment and Automation
5. Master Bus Processing and Tweaks
6. Multi-environment Listening and Final Tweaks
7. Wrap-up and Housekeeping

Mommy, how long does a mix take?

One of the questions I'm asked frequently, by both clients and students, is, "how long will it take you to mix a song?" I often respond with, "How long will it take you to *write* a song?" The point here is that there's no way to know in advance exactly how long a part of the creative process is going to take. Sure, there are ballparks and guidelines, but when it comes to mixing, there are many factors that affect the time it takes, not the least of which are the number of tracks and the condition of the audio. A song with 30 pristine tracks is very different from a song with 8 tracks full of hisses, buzzes and bad punch-ins. Over time, I've gotten fairly accurate at ballparking how long a song might take to mix, *but only after I've checked out the tracks*. Even then, a mix is going to take as long as it requires, and mixing two different songs is never the same – just as the process of writing two songs is never the same.

Use and re-use

As we discussed earlier, one of the most wonderful things about mixing "in the box" is *replicability*. In addition to allowing us to spit out a mix that will sound absolutely identical every time we render it, replicability also allows us to re-use things over and over again, from mix to mix. If you have a collection of similarly-recorded songs to mix, you might follow every step in this methodology to a T on the first song, but once you've got it in the can, you've got a TON of stuff you can use as starting points for the rest of the songs in the collection. For example, if you have songs that were recorded by a band at the same place and time, chances are the same mics were used – in the same configuration – for the drum kit on every song. That means that all that hard work (and time!) you put into getting the kick, snare, hat, overheads and toms dialed in just right on the first song should work pretty darn well as a drum foundation for the next song, even if you end up making small adjustments for variations in song style, playing intensity, etc. And the same goes for all of the other tracks the band recorded. As a result, it might take you X hours to mix Song 1, but only half or a third of that time to mix Song 2. By the time you get to Song 10, you'll have such a great palate of starting points to choose from that it might only take you a quarter of the time it took to mix Song 1.

I employ this re-use technique on every multi-song project that I mix. Sometimes I can even use it between projects that I've recorded at my own studio, because I tend to follow a pretty consistent process when recording, just as I do with mixing. On a multi-song project, the first thing I do after finishing the first mix (and after making a backup, of course!) is export the settings for every track, group, effect and the master bus to the song's project folder, and name the resulting files accordingly. Cubase and Nuendo have a fantastic feature that allows me to export and import the settings for a collection of as many different types of tracks, groups, etc. as I choose as a single file. For example, I can export all of the settings for the drums into a single file that I'll name "Drums - 12 mono tracks, 6 stereo groups.xml." Then, assuming I arrange the drum tracks in the same order in the next song, I can select that same combination of tracks and groups in the new song, simply import my "Drums - 12 mono tracks, 6 stereo groups.xml" file and voila! Instant setup for 18 channels of drums, with every setting intact. It's an enormous time saver that I couldn't imagine living without. If

8

your DAW software offers anything remotely like this, use it! The more songs you mix as a collection, the more valuable it will be.

Another factor that's going to affect how long it takes you to mix a song is your *experience*. If you've mixed 300 songs instead of 30, you'll likely need less time on average to mix a given song. Similarly, if you've been using your DAW and plug-ins for two years instead of two weeks, you're bound to know your way around, have some go-to plug-ins and saved presets, and have developed a number of time-saving shortcuts in your use of the software.

Finally, it call comes back around to where we started: if you develop a rock-solid, well-defined mixing process and methodology (such as the one presented here) that you follow fairly religiously, I'm absolutely sure you'll get faster (and as a bonus, better-sounding) mixes.

Phase 1: Environment Setup

There's a "phase" that needs to be addressed before we jump into the "official" stages of the mixing process. More than an actual phase, it's more of a *state* that our stuff needs to be in for the subsequent phases to go smoothly. This all might seem a little dry or tedious, but we need to start at the beginning if we're going to get it right down the line, so we might as well get it out of the way here.

Data organization and consistency

One of the things I had to learn the hard way was that all of the data we use in the mixing process needs to be extremely well organized. And "data" is more than just mix project files and tracks. It includes folder structures, plug-in presets, client e-mails and notes, and lots of other supporting information. Proper organization of this data becomes more critical the more clients you have, but the concepts apply even if you only mix a lot of your own material. In addition, whatever process of organization you adopt, it also has to be *consistent*.

Naming consistency

At a minimum, it's essential to arrange and name things consistently, if for no other reason than to be able to find things quickly when you need them. For example, decide whether you want to name your client folders by [Firstname Lastname] or [Lastname, Firstname] and then make sure to name them all the same way, and not mix and match. The same goes for whatever conventions you adopt for the use of upper- and lower-case letters, underscores, dashes, and spaces, and they should be consistent across project names, track names, plug-in presets – basically anything that needs to be organized in some fashion. These guidelines apply for any written/printed information as well as files stored on computer.

Drive and folder structure

Here's how I arrange all of my studio data: On my main control room computer, I have three primary hard drives. The first is called "System" and it's where my operating system, executable programs and related files reside. The second is called "Projects" and contains everything to do with my music projects. The third hard drive is called "Backups" and is used for immediate, first-level backups of all of the projects I work on. Depending on the project, I may also have one or more other hard drives connected to the system that contain other things, such as the content for virtual instrument libraries (mostly for efficiency reasons, I don't keep that information on the System drive).

Here's a screenshot of my main control room computer (which happens to be called "AMD1100T") showing its connected hard drives.

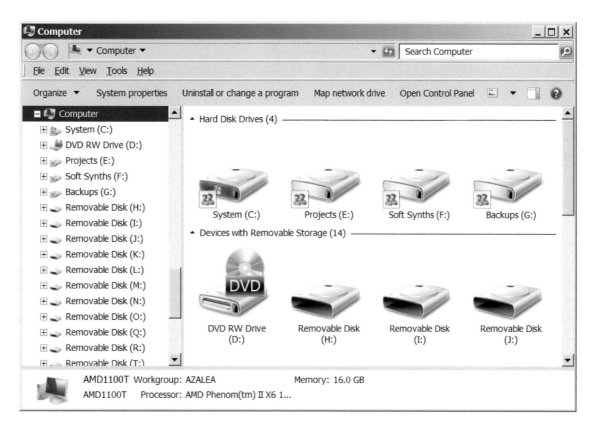

Project drive/Client Files folder

Needless to say, the Project drive is the heart and soul of everything I do (and how I make my living), so keeping it well organized and treating it with kid gloves is critical. The main folder on the Project drive is called "Client Files" and is arranged in alphabetically-named folders for each client, by last name and first name (e.g., "Moran, Nancy"). Having the Client Files folder arranged this way keeps all of my clients' projects separated from one another, and also makes it possible to find things really, really quickly. If you're a home-studio owner and work exclusively on your own projects, you don't technically need a "Client Files" folder or a sub-folder with your name in it, but I still recommend using them because, on the outside chance that you ever decide to do a project for someone else, then you'll already have a structure in place to distinguish your stuff from theirs without having to make any changes. Folders unto themselves don't really use any drive space to speak of, so it doesn't hurt to put these two "placeholder" folders into your structure. If you do use this structure for your own stuff, one of the folders under Client Files will be your own Lastname, Firstname. At a minimum, I would recommend using something like "Project Files" in place of the "Client Files" folder, so you'll be able to distinguish all of your project-related stuff from any other top-level folders – which you'll inevitably have – on your Projects drive.

Here's a screenshot of the "Client Files" folder on my Project drive, showing a separate folder for each client, named by Lastname, Firstname (except in a few cases where the client is a company or other organization).

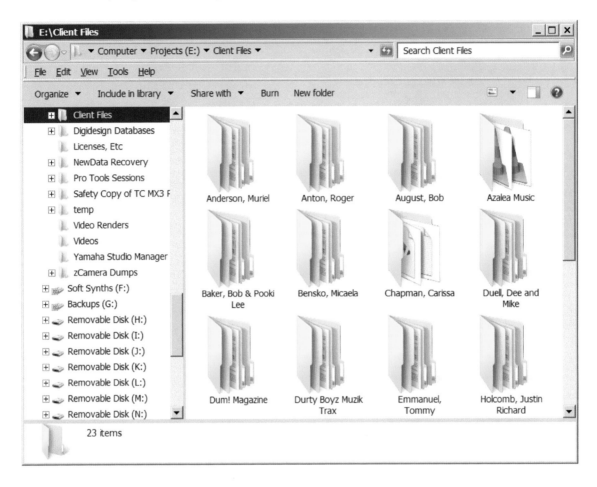

In my setup, under each client's main folder is a folder structure that I use consistently for every client. It looks like this:

Client Files
    [Lastname, Firstname]
        Cubase Projects (and/or Pro Tools Projects, SONAR Projects, Logic Projects, etc.)
            [Songname1]
            [Songname2]
            ...etc...
        Files To Be Sent
            Files Already Sent
        Imported Files
        Mixes, Etc
            Processed Files

Encoded Files
Work Versions, Lyrics, Etc

(FYI, the folder names in square brackets ([]) above vary by situation; the rest of the folder names are literal.)

Arranging my client folders this way puts everything at my fingertips, and matches my work flow as well. I've tried numerous versions of this structure over the years, and this is the one that has stuck (and worked extremely well) for quite a while now. If you don't already have some kind of consistent folder structure, I strongly recommend setting this one up, putting your files into it, and trying it out. It may take a while to get comfortable with, but it's definitely better than no structure at all. If you already have a pretty good structure of your own that works well for you, you don't have to use this one; the point is to have a structure in place and use it consistently. You'll be accessing it constantly, and it's the first place to avoid clutter and potential trip-ups in the middle of mixing a project because things have been misplaced.

Here's a screenshot showing the underlying structure of the folder for a single client (Roger Anton).

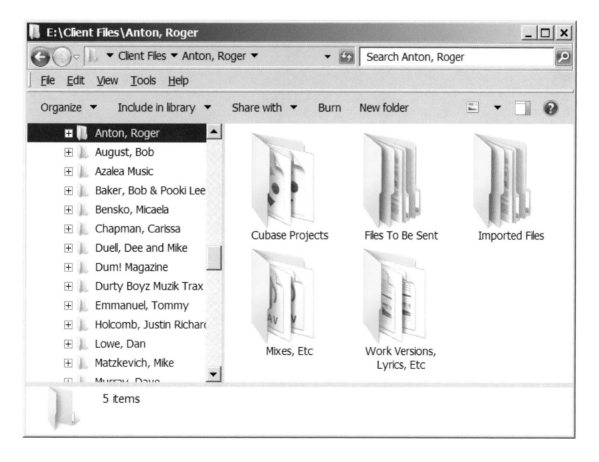

DAW projects folders

The first folder in the example above is "Cubase Projects." Note that, because of all the different clients and other studios I work with, I use a number of different DAWs, so I might have different instances of these DAW-named "Projects" folders under different clients. (FYI, I'm an admittedly huge fan of Cubase, and it's what I always choose first if it's up to me. That's the only reason the screenshot examples in this book are from Cubase; they could just as well have been from any other DAW.) Typically, each client tends to work in only one DAW, so I might have a "Pro Tools Projects" folder under one client and a "Nuendo Projects" folder under another client, but rarely more than one for a single client. If you're a home studio owner and work exclusively on your own material, chances are you probably use just one DAW, but if you do, I still recommend that you have an aptly-named DAW folder for it. It helps to keep your DAW project files arranged separately from everything else, and avoids clutter. Also, if you ever do find yourself working in another DAW, you'll already have a structure in place that it will fit right into, and you won't have to rearrange any of your existing files.

The following screenshot shows the contents of a client's DAW projects folder (in client Roger Anton's case, "Cubase Projects") that contains project files for two songs.

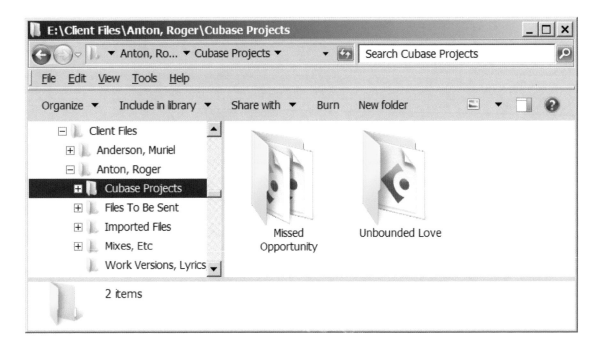

Song folders

Under the DAW folder (e.g., "Cubase Projects") I arrange everything by song name. There's a very important implication here that I consider a song and a DAW project file to be on an equal level, or to put it another way, a DAW project file is the embodiment of one and only one song, rather than multiple songs in a music project. (Just to be clear, what I mean by a "DAW project file" is .cpr for Cubase, .pts for Pro Tools, .cwp for SONAR, .lso for Logic, etc.) One of the biggest mistakes I see with some of my home-studio clients is that *all* of their project files, for *every* song (and therefore, all of their multi-track data files) are in one place, usually the top level of a hard drive. Not only is this organizationally frustrating, it also means that ALL of the audio tracks for ALL of the songs reside together in a single folder (most DAWs have an "Audio" folder or equivalent just under the project level)! If you do things this way, when you're looking at the Audio folder, there is absolutely no way to tell which songs the files "Bass_01" and "Bass_16" belong to. They could belong to the same song or two different songs. If you ever have to do any kind of recovery or reconstruction of your Project drive, it will be a nightmare. For these reasons, I never, ever mix and match songs (and their DAW project files) in the same folder; EVERY SONG GETS ITS OWN FOLDER.

Here's a screenshot of the folder for a single song. In this case, there are two Cubase (.cpr) project files, reflecting the first two steps in getting the song ready to mix.

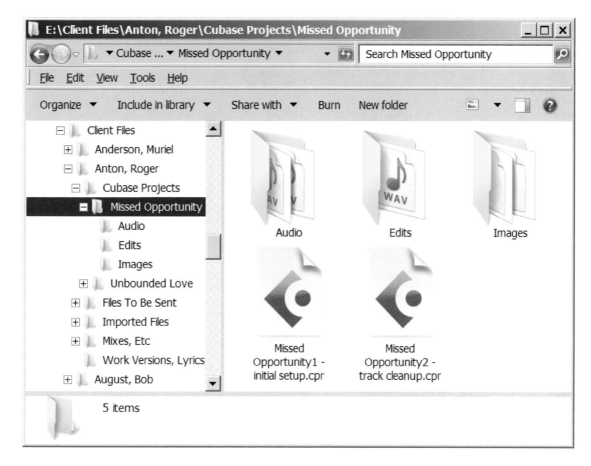

DAW-owned folders

Under each song's folder, as projects are created, the corresponding DAW software will create other sub-folders for its project-related supporting files, typically things like

"Audio," "Images," "Edits," "Fades" and the like. Since these files are created automatically and vary by DAW, I haven't specified them in the structure above. Just know that they're going to be there, and don't ever, ever move or rename them – they "belong" to the DAW software, so hands off!

Imported Files folder

In my folder structure above, another key folder is the "Imported Files" folder. This is where I put all of the files I receive FROM the client – i.e., files they've created externally and sent to me. Once I place a client's files in this folder, I leave them there and always use *copies* of them in my projects. The main reason is that if I ever have a problem, I can always revert to the client's originals and know that they haven't been modified in any way. This folder also makes it easy for me to know what a client has sent me (and what they haven't) during the course of a project.

Here's a screenshot of our client's "Imported Files" folder, which contains a single ZIP archive of some files we received from him.

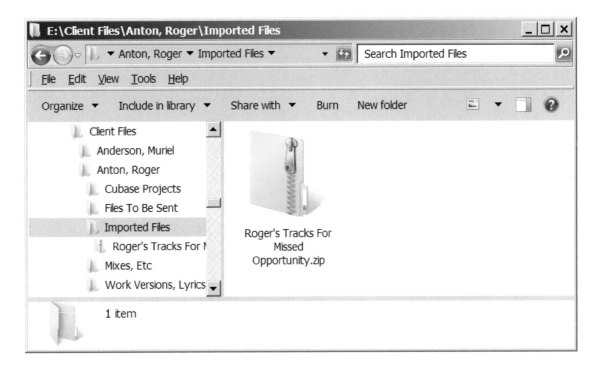

Files To Be Sent folder

While not totally necessary, you may also want to keep a folder called "Files To Be Sent" under each client as well. Using the same logic as the "Imported Files" folder, if you place *copies* of files you intend to send to the client (e.g., MP3s of finished mixes) in this folder, you'll be able keep track of what you have and haven't sent them. As an added measure, you can also create a sub-folder under "Files To Be Sent" called "Files Already Sent" where you can put files that you've already taken care of, for reference/record-keeping. Using this structure, you automatically know at a glance that any files residing at the "Files To Be Sent" folder level still need your attention.

Mixes, Etc folder

The next folder in the hierarchy (and this is a biggie, second only to the DAW projects folders) is the "Mixes, Etc" folder (by convention, I don't bother putting the period at the end of "Etc" here, as it serves absolutely no linguistic purpose in this context and just causes clutter). As the name implies, this folder contains mixes *and anything that is generated from them*, such as mastered mixes, MP3s, CD montage files from WaveLab (my mastering platform of choice), etc. This implies that I keep my DAW project files (from which I create mixes) in a separate folder than the mixes that result. Many people like to keep their mixes under the DAW project's Audio or Exports folder (or equivalent) so that all files relating to a song are in the same place under the song itself. You're welcome to do this (in which case you might not have a Mixes, Etc folder), but I find it cumbersome. My logic is that I mix one song at a time, but I deal with multiple mixes together when sending to the client, mastering, preparing a CD, etc., so working with project files and mixes are two completely different activities with different purposes for me. If I want to send five mixes to a client, I don't want to have to go looking through five different DAW projects' Audio folders to find them; I'd much rather they were all in one place, so I can work with them as a set. Depending on the size of a client project, or how many projects I do with them over time, I may start sub-dividing the Mixes, Etc folder into sub-folders by album title, song name, or the like, but whether you go to this level of separation or not, the point is that ALL of the mix (and related) files are still under one common folder, and not spread among other stuff.

Here's a screenshot of Roger Anton's "Mixes, Etc" Folder.

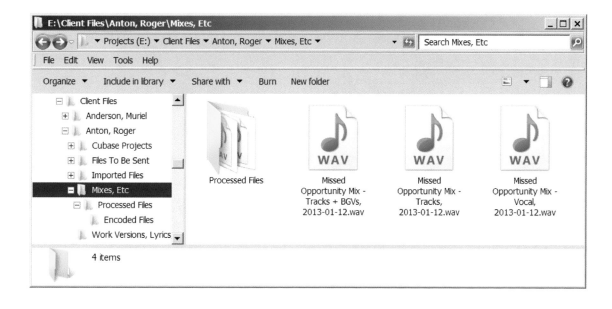

Processed Files folder

The bulk of the files in the Mixes, Etc folder will be stereo WAV or AIF files that are the result of "renders" or "exports" from DAW projects. Under the Mixes, Etc folder is a sub-folder called "Processed Files." This is where I put mastered files and the like. As the folder name implies, these are files that come after initial mix exporting/rendering, and have some kind of after-the-fact processing (mastering EQ/compression/limiting, resampling, dithering, loudness normalization, etc.) applied to them. Part of the reason I use this structure is to separate steps in the work process, but it also makes it easy to go backwards to the original, un-processed mix and start over if I need to, or make different versions from the same starting point, or make comparisons between pre-processed and post-processed versions. I name the files at the various stages of processing accordingly.

Here's Roger's "Processed Files" folder. The "M-" and "DBLat-10-" file prefixes are part of a naming scheme I use when I master songs.

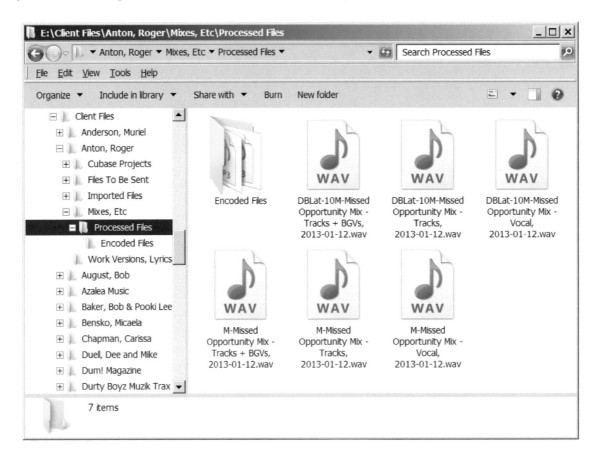

Encoded Files folder

Finally, under the "Processed Files" folder is a folder called "Encoded Files." This is optional, but I find it easier to keep things organized. Again, as the name suggests, the files in this folder are mastered (or otherwise processed) mixes that have been encoded into some other format than the original, most commonly MP3, AAC, WMA and FLAC. By having this extra level of folder for these files, I can simply work my way up and down the hierarchy to get to the files I need from any stage of the mixing/mastering/encoding process. If you want to get really crazy, you can have separate folders for each encoded format, but in my experience, most clients and projects usually need only one.

Here's a screenshot of Roger's "Encoded Files" folder.

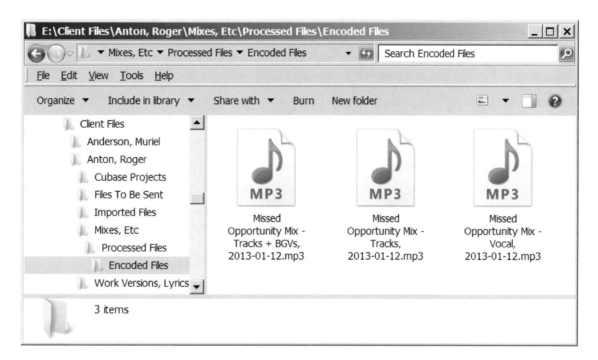

What about client- or song-specific presets?

Logic (the thought process, not the DAW program from Apple) would dictate that you'd also want to store any kind of presets for plug-ins and the like that you use for a specific client or song in this folder hierarchy. You might decide to keep safety/backup copies of such files here, but in my experience, most plug-in software prefers (or demands) that presets be stored under its own hierarchy, wherever the software has been installed (typically the System drive), so that's where I store them. HOWEVER, for plug-in software that allows me to do it, I do create sub-folders for specific clients and songs under the software's "Presets" folder, to make them easier to find.

Unfortunately, software companies are inconsistent in their folder structure, so we don't always have control over how we get to use it. Do whatever you can to be as organized as possible under a given companies' preset hierarchy, but I don't recommend storing presets in your Client Files hierarchy even if the software lets you.

Here's an example of a presets folder "owned" by a third-party plug-in (in this case, TC Electronic's MasterX3, part of TC's PowerCore series). You'll notice that the plug-in stores the preset hierarchy under the "My Documents" folder. This is a choice made by the plug-in at installation, not by the user.

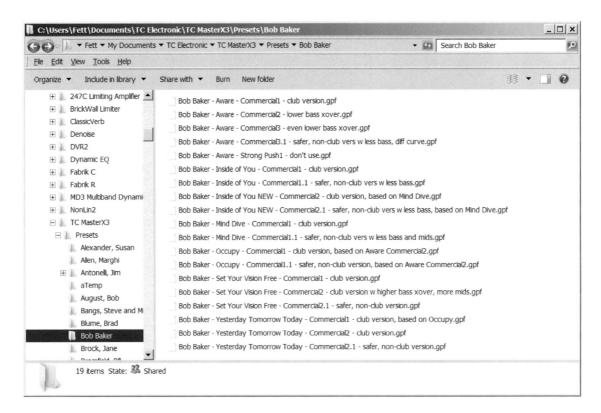

Last but not least, I've got a folder under each client called "Work Versions, Lyrics, Etc." These files are different from those in the "Imported Files" folder in that they're not actually used in recording, mixing, or mastering, but are there for background and reference to the overall music production process. For example, if you're recording a demo for a client, they might have sent you a guitar-vocal "work version" (reference recording) in an MP3, along with some suggested production notes, lyrics for you and a demo singer, and possibly one or more charts for the musicians. That stuff all goes here. Note that, even though these files aren't part of the final recording, they need to be here at your fingertips so you can find information in the moment ("what was that vocal phrasing in the third line again…?"), and not buried in e-mails on your laptop or smartphone, even if you also have copies there. Trust me: you'll be happy you did it this way.

Here's a screenshot of our client's "Work Versions, Lyrics, Etc" folder.

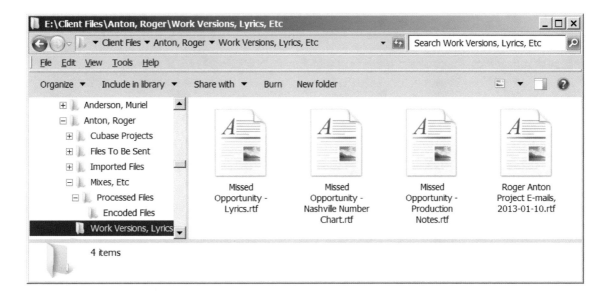

That wasn't so bad, was it? With this folder structure in place, you'll be armed and ready to take on any size project with ease, so if you haven't done so and don't already have your own structure in place, take the time to set things up this way now, before you start creating a bunch of random folders and files on your hard drive. They have a tendency to proliferate and overwhelm us pretty quickly if we're not prepared in advance. Yep, learned that one the hard way.

Okay, we're prepared for the "official" phases of the mixing process, so let's rock…

Phase 2: Mix setup and maintenance

This phase is an entirely non-musical part of the mixing process. Ideally, you want to get all of these mechanical, left-brain tasks out of the way in one go, at the beginning, rather than doing them in-between the other, musically-oriented mixing steps later. It makes for faster, better mixes, and keeps you from having to constantly switch your mind between left-brain and right-brain activities, which can be exhausting.

Create project (or use existing one)

You can do a mix from either an existing project file that already contains the music tracks (e.g., one previously used to track and overdub the song), or a brand-new project file (or template) into which you import contiguous audio or MIDI files into fresh tracks. This is a matter of preference and working style; either one is fine. For songs that I both record and mix, I tend to evolve the same project file throughout the life of the song, saving many times under a new name as I progress through the process. If I didn't record the song and am just mixing it for a client, I'll start with a template into which I load the client's files.

Save and back up as you go!

Whichever method you choose, from here on out, you're going to want to do a "save as" to a newly-named file *after every significant change that you make to the mix*. I can't stress enough how following this methodology will save you countless headaches down the line. A typical collection of project files I have by the time I've finished mixing a single song can number in the double digits. That's perfectly fine, and project files (as opposed to audio files) take up miniscule amounts of space. The reason I so strongly recommend creating incremental "save as" files is that, if you suddenly realize that you've royally hosed something in the previous twenty minutes or fifty changes (or worse yet, the project file you're working on suddenly becomes corrupted and unusable by your DAW – it does happen!), the only work you'll lose is whatever you've done since your last "save as." You can simply go back to that file and pick up where you left off. That's far more palatable than having every change you've made to the mix since the beginning saved in one file, with no idea how far back to go. Yes, "undo" can help, but only since the last time you opened the file. You'd be surprised at how many changes you can make to a mix in a few hours; the thought of losing all of that work because you have to go so far back can be heart-wrenching at best. In the space of a few hours, I'll typically save about a half-dozen incremental project files as I mix, which means I'll never lose more than about a half-hour of work, worst case.

Here's an illustration of what I mean... Say I've been mixing a song and I'm several steps into the process. My list of project files (if I'm using Cubase) will look something like this:

Down By The River Mix1 - after initial file load.cpr
Down By The River Mix2 - after import of channel settings and presets.cpr
Down By The River Mix3 - after tracks cleaned up and trimmed.cpr
Down By The River Mix4 - after basic dial-in of drums.cpr
Down By The River Mix5 - continuing with drums.cpr
Down By The River Mix6 - drums dialed in, adding bass.cpr

And so on. You can see how the number of project files can proliferate quite quickly. And that's *exactly what you want*. Using this methodology, you never have many changes in a single project file. I use the combination of song name and number for two reasons: first, it gives me a really obvious view of the logical order of changes; and two, it always sorts in the correct order if I view the list of files by file name. As a convention, I follow the number by a dash separated by spaces, and an obvious, lowercase description of the set of changes, so the file names are super-easy to read at a glance.

Here's a real-world example of a bunch of successively-named project files throughout the course of a mixing project:

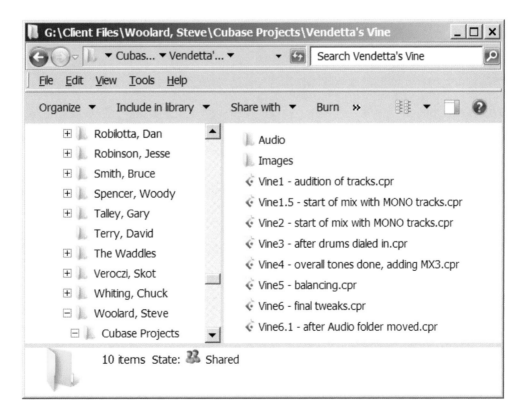

Similarly, every time you finish a major round of mixing (e.g., every few hours), I strongly recommend making a backup copy of your changes on some local drive of your choosing, for disaster recovery. Believe it or not, I have actually had my main Project drive go belly-up in the middle of mixing a song. Ever since then, I've kept a separate "Backups" hard drive connected to my control room machine that has a folder called "Client Backups From Projects." After every major mixing session, I copy the files I've been working on to a correspondingly-named client folder on that drive, and save them under a folder named by date.

Here's an example:

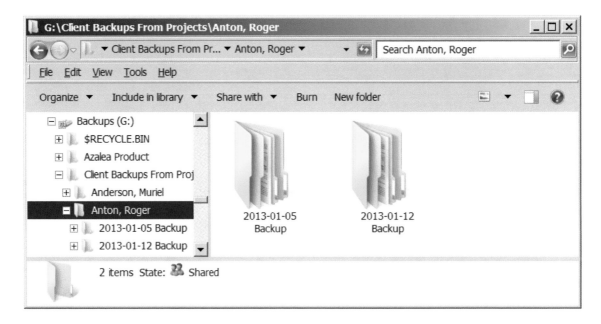

By following this process, not only can you never lose more than a few hours' work on a project, you're also able to get back up and running fairly quickly if your main Project drive becomes toast; and I can guarantee you, someday it will.

Everyone's threshold of pain is different; how often you create incremental "save as" project files and back them up to a separate drive depends on how much work you are willing to have to completely do over, or worst case (assuming you can't remember all the changes you've made), lose forever. Paranoia can be your friend here! ☺

Import files to tracks (or use existing ones)

Note: most of what we cover in this section applies to both audio and MIDI, so when I say things like "rename all tracks" or "import files," I'm referring to both.

If you are importing files, ideally you want to use contiguous files that all start at the same relative time location so that there are no potential issues with different parts not lining up. This approach is much more preferable than importing a bunch of small audio snippets and hoping they're all time-stamped correctly (e.g., as Broadcast WAV files). Of course, if you're starting with an existing project that already contains the audio data, then this issue is not a consideration.

Whether importing to fresh tracks or using existing ones, this is the time to correctly name/label the tracks in terms of their musical function in the mix, rather than their mechanical function in the project. For example, this is the point to, if you haven't done so during recording and overdubbing, rename tracks "Audio01" and "Audio02" to "AcGtr1-Neck" and "AcGtr1-Body" or such. I find that a combination of initial caps and lowercase letters (e.g., "AcGtr1") rather than lowercase and underscores (e.g., "ac_gtr_1") is easier to read, and uses less precious screen space (underscores take up extra characters). Use names that are musically logical and descriptive – not just to you, but to anyone else who might potentially end up using your mix project sometime in the future. You'll be glad you did!

Here's a screenshot from a Cubase project that illustrates what I'm talking about. In this case, the two guitar tracks are labeled "L" and "R" (for Left and Right) rather than "Neck" and "Body," but the concept applies regardless of the specific naming convention.

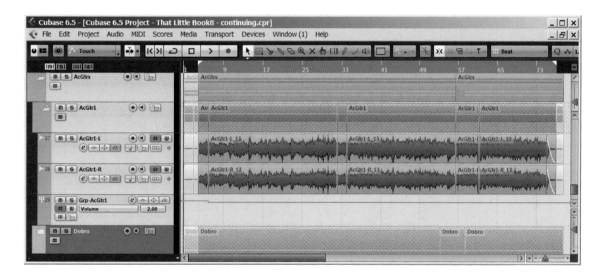

Just to be clear, I'm talking about renaming *tracks* and *channels* here, NOT their underlying audio or MIDI files. You NEVER want to rename your audio or MIDI files. They're the exclusive domain of your DAW, so let it name and manage them for you. This might mean that you end up with a *track* named "AcGtr1-Neck" that refers to a *file* named "Audio01_13." That's okay. While it would have been better to correctly name tracks before recording, when you're at the mixing stage, what you should be spending the bulk of your time looking at is the tracks, not their underlying files, so you want good, mnemonic track names.

Group tracks by instrumental and vocal "parts"

Whether importing files to fresh tracks or starting with existing tracks, this is the point at which you want to start thinking of groups of tracks as musical *parts* rather than simply as individual linear waveforms on the screen. For example, if you have two mics on an acoustic guitar, those two tracks should be physically located together on the screen, and assigned together to a group track as a single guitar *part*. For parts that involve only a single track, like bass guitar, there's really no reason to create a group. But for anything that is multi-miked or otherwise recorded onto multiple tracks (e.g., acoustic guitars, guitar amps, drums, keyboards) or performed as an ensemble (e.g., backing vocals, horns, string sections), you'll want to create a group and assign the individual tracks to that group. This takes surprisingly little time once you get the hang of it, especially if you use track templates or similar tools to easily duplicate repetitive tasks.

Just to be clear, I use the term "groups" here to describe *aggregate tracks that receive audio from one or more other tracks*. Different DAWs use different terms for these (e.g., a group is called an "Aux" in Pro Tools); I use the term "groups" because I'm historically a Cubase/Nuendo guy and that's what they call them, but also because the term reminds me that several things are functionally "grouped" together and manipulated as such.

Stereo vs. mono groups

You'll want to use stereo groups instead of mono groups if there is even a remote chance that contributing tracks might be panned within the group. Otherwise, mono is fine (and can use less computer resources on plug-ins that offer mono versions).

Make sure to name/label your groups logically just as you did the individual tracks that are assigned to them. For example, if you have two tracks named "AcGtr1-Neck" and "AcGtr1-Body" you'll want to name their group something like "Grp-AcGtr1" to show that they're related. Note that I put "Grp-" in the front of my group tracks' names. This might seem redundant, but depending on which DAW software you use, it may not be easy to distinguish between individual audio and MIDI tracks and group tracks at a glance. Having "Grp-" at the beginning of group tracks uses only a few characters and leaves no doubt – you'll know that's where you'll make most of your adjustments, not on the individual tracks assigned to then.

In addition to co-locating related tracks together on the screen, I also co-locate the group to which they're assigned directly below them, so that I can see/manipulate them all as a unit. In DAWs like Cubase/Nuendo that have the concept of "Folder" tracks, I'll put all of the individual tracks and their group together in their own folder that I name accordingly as well, creating a hierarchy like this:

Folder Track: AcGtr1
       Audio Track: AcGtr1-Neck
       Audio Track: AcGtr1-Body
       Group Track: Grp-AcGtr1

Here's that screenshot of the acoustic guitar and its associated audio tracks and groups again. Everything to do with "AcGtr1" is similarly named and located together in one place in the project.

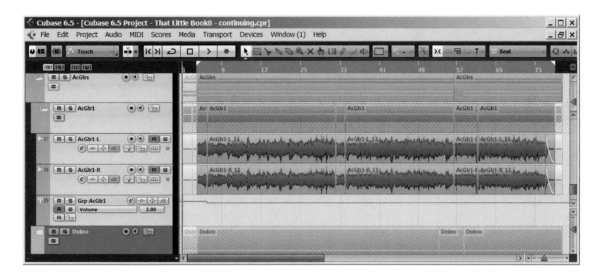

As an aside, I often capture both audio and MIDI output from external keyboards when recording; when I have both audio and MIDI data for the same part, I group them together in the project so I know they go together. It also makes it easy for me switch between the audio and MIDI when deciding which to use (or both together) when mixing the part.

Here's an example, and a screenshot from a real-world implementation:

Folder Track: Piano
       Audio Track: Piano-L
       Audio Track: Piano-R
       MIDI Track: Piano
       Group Track: Grp-Piano

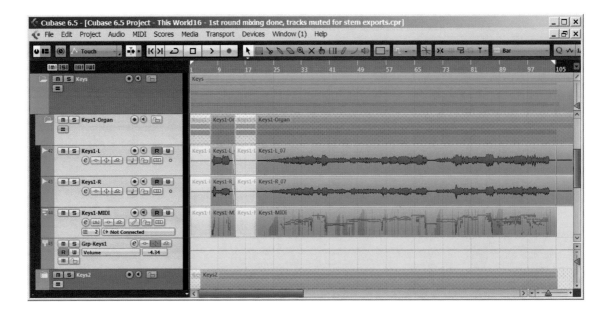

Using folders in this manner makes it easy to edit, mute, solo and otherwise manipulate each "part" in the arrangement very easily. In programs like Cubase and Nuendo, folders also allow you to do global edits on multiple, related tracks (e.g., drums) at the same time, which can save tons of time and cut down on inadvertent editing errors.

There's another key reason to use groups besides simple organization. During mixing, most of the processing will be applied to the group for each part, rather than to each individual track that feeds the group, resulting in an enormous savings in computer resources. For example, rather than adding compression and reverb to both the neck and body tracks of an acoustic guitar, most of the time, we can assign both tracks to an acoustic guitar group, and apply the compression and reverb there only once. That uses half as much memory, CPU cycles, etc. for processing the part.

Add colors to tracks/parts

This is the point at which to use color to further distinguish all of your tracks as parts of an *arrangement*. You can either make all of a part's tracks (folder, audio, MIDI, group, etc.) the same color, or make them some mix of related colors – whatever makes it easiest for you to "see" the part easily. However you decide to do it, make sure you're consistent with your use of colors throughout the project (and ideally, from project to project); it will save you time when mixing. Templates make the process a one-time, set-and-forget exercise.

Here's a screenshot showing our keyboard part along with two other, different keyboard parts in the same song. The color really makes it easy to zero in on a specific keyboard part at a glance.

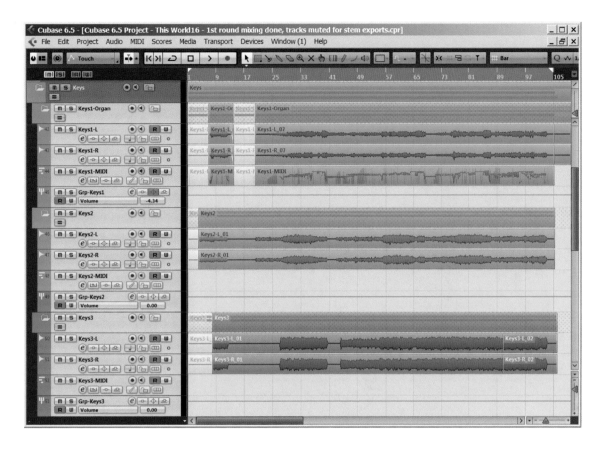

Here's another screenshot of various folders containing the tracks for a bunch of different parts in a Cubase project. The use of color really helps to identify things quickly – especially in a complex mix with a lot of parts and tracks.

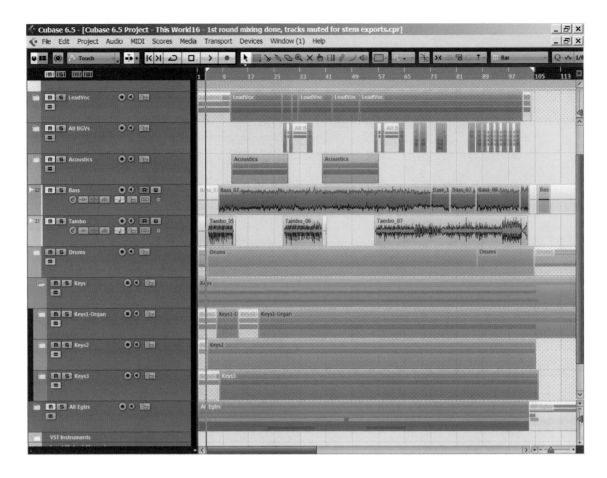

This is probably a great time to do a "save as" and possibly a backup! ☺

Trim space from/clean up tracks

The first part of this step involves trimming the heads and tails (start and end) of all tracks so that both the beginning and the end of the song are as "clean" as possible. You want to start each track at the point where the instrument or voice starts to perform, and remove any noise or other distractions (noisy guitar amps, vocal sniffles, etc.) at this point. Don't make your edits/cuts too close. If your DAW allows for it, maximize the view of the tracks' waveforms so you can really see what's there so you don't inadvertently cut off any audio.

Here's a screenshot of our acoustic guitar part with heads and tails trimmed. The very front and end parts of the tracks have been muted out completely (shown in white).

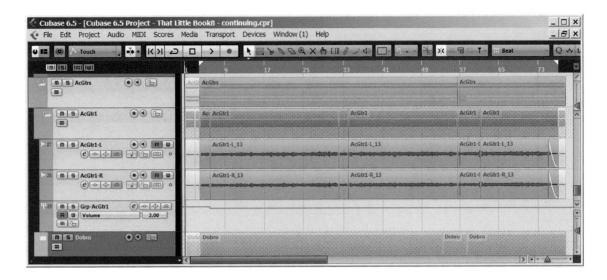

Here's a screenshot of the same tracks, with the waveforms enlarged to show more detail for editing.

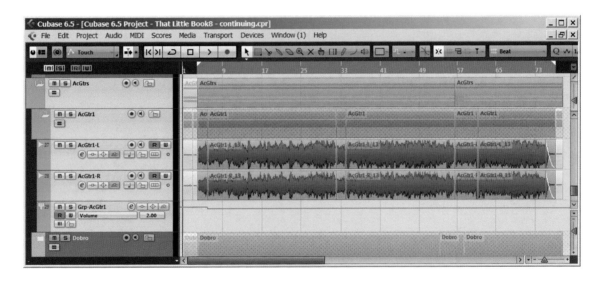

To make things sound natural, you might need to add a small fade-in at the beginning or fade-out at the end on a track. It's worth taking the time to do this now, because as you add EQ, compression, effects, etc. later during the mixing process, these little distractions will become much more noticeable and annoying, and you don't want to have to switch to left-brain editing mode in the middle of mixing to tend to them. Get it over with now!

Here are close-ups of the fade-in and fade-out added at the beginning and end of the guitar tracks, which make our edits smoother and unnoticeable on playback.

31

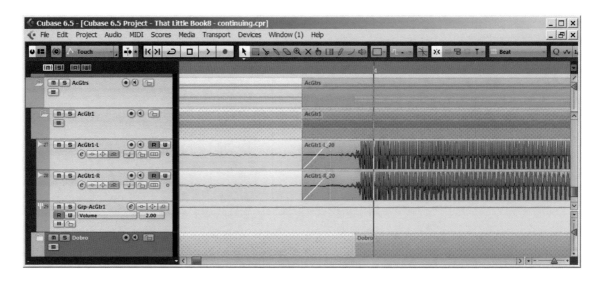

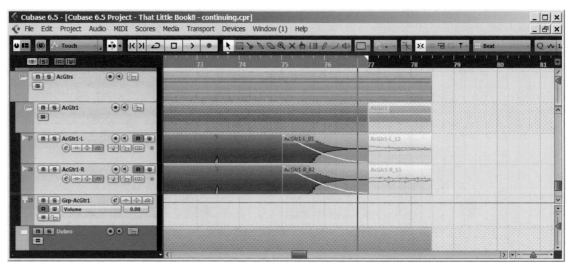

In addition to trimming the start and end of each track, I recommend that you visually cut out longer spaces where instruments aren't playing or vocalists aren't singing. I think this part is critical. In my experience, it saves time and helps you to start thinking of the various instrumental and vocal parts of the song as an arrangement. You can literally *see* when parts come in and out during the course of the song. It also makes it easier to mute, change levels, add processing, etc. to parts based on *sections of the song*, rather than as individual tracks. Yes, simply muting sections with automation accomplishes the same sonic result, but it doesn't give you that immediate, visual picture of the song's arrangement and structure. So take the time to do it; with today's DAW editing tools, it really doesn't take very long.

Here's a screenshot of a bunch of BGV (background vocal) tracks that have been trimmed to only the places where there's actual singing. It's easy to tell where the BGVs take place in the arrangement of the song.

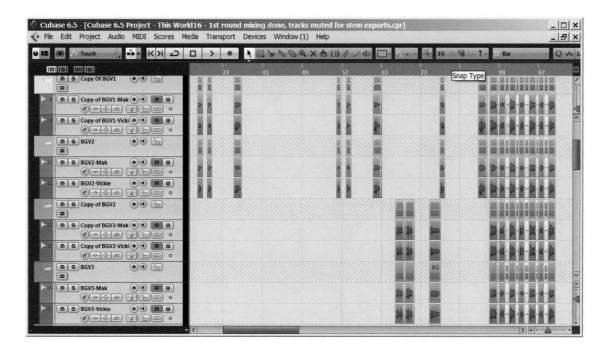

This is also the time to tend to any "sonic surgery" on tracks that you already know need to be cleaned up or fixed in some way. For example, tracks that were recorded at extremely low volume might need to be normalized in order to have enough volume to be usable in the mix. If there are any known digital snaps, crackles and pops on any tracks, this is the time to clean them up – *before* you start mixing in earnest.

Comp tracks

This is the point at which to "comp" (i.e., make contiguous, "composite" performances of) tracks together – NOT later as you encounter them while mixing. That's because comping – just like track cleanup – is a technical, left-brain activity and not a musical, right-brain activity. Comping in the middle of mixing will force you to unnecessarily switch headspaces and get out of "musical mode," which you want to avoid.

This is the time to go through parts (especially vocals) and decide exactly which combination of takes and snippets of audio you want to use for the complete, "final" part in the mix. It's also the time to create (if necessary) and clean up any cross-fades between the various snippets of audio in the comped part, or, if you're starting with the project file that was used for recording, anywhere punch-ins were done.

Here are a couple of screenshots showing a cross-fade edit between two snippets of audio on our acoustic guitar tracks. The second screenshot shows the benefit of increasing the view of the waveform to see what's really going on with the audio at the point of the cross-fade.

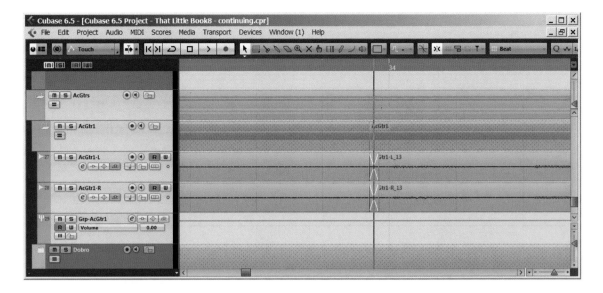

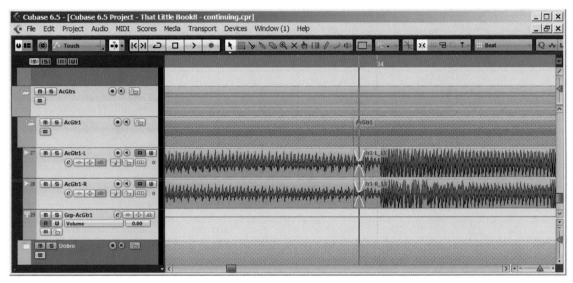

The goal by the end of this process is to *never have to think of or manipulate the individual audio snippets again*, but only the entire part as it was played or sung, from start to finish. Especially for tracks with lots of comped audio snippets, one way to help yourself think this way is to consolidate the comped part to a new track in the project that is aptly named (e.g., "LeadVoc-COMPED") and then turn off/disable/hide the original track(s) from which the comp was made. Some DAWs make it easy to do this automatically on an existing track (e.g., the "Events to Part" function in Cubase/Nuendo); worst case, you'll simply export/render/bounce the original track to a file and then import the file to a new track. Regardless of how you do it, this consolidation helps to save computer resources, and is especially good practice if you intend to pitch-adjust a part later; you can do the pitch adjustments on this contiguous, comped track, not the original snippets.

Here are some screenshots showing the processing of comping a lead vocal part. First, we comp the vocal on the original audio track. In this example, we've comped the vocal using Cubase's Lanes feature and its Comp Tool.

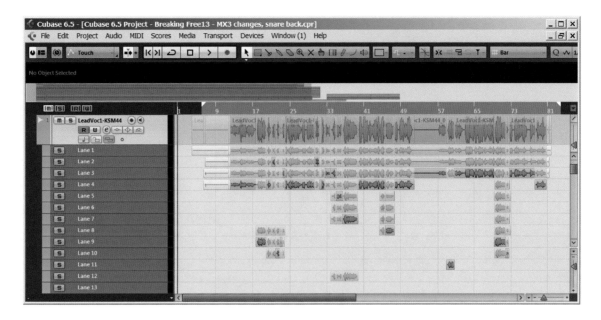

Next, we export the original, comped track to a new one that contains only the results of the comp, rather than all the original snippets of audio. We'll use this new track as the basis for any further manipulation we do on the lead vocal (e.g., pitch adjustment).

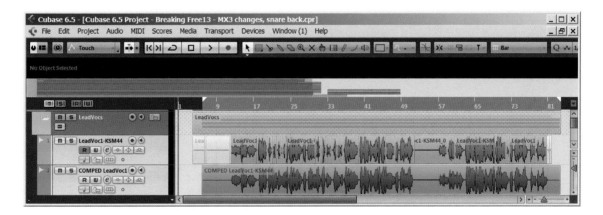

Pitch-adjust tracks

Like comping, pitch adjustment is a mechanical, left-brain activity, and this is the time to get it out of the way. But only do it if you NEED to; don't pitch-adjust anything if it's not really *musically* necessary. I'm not a big fan of pitch adjustment – not because I'm afraid of the technology or have some extreme moral aversion to it, but rather, because 99% of the time, no matter how skillfully it's applied or by whom, it's audible in the finished product, and usually not in a good way.

If you absolutely MUST pitch-adjust a part for musical reasons, then pitch-adjust only those individual notes or small sections that actually need it, and leave the rest of the part "au naturel." If you do, you'll have much less chance of the pitch adjustment being noticed in the final result, because the small pieces that are pitch-adjusted will be very brief and go by quickly during playback. Today's pitch adjustment software makes it very easy to "grab" the tiniest section of a part and apply processing to only that section, so there's no excuse for not taking the time to do it this way.

As mentioned above, I recommend doing the pitch adjustment on a contiguous, comped track rather than on a bunch of individual snippets that eventually go into a comp. It's much easier to keep track of what's what when you only have one contiguous piece of audio to work on.

As with comping, once pitch adjustment is done, I recommend rendering/exporting the combination of pitch-adjusted and un-adjusted parts into a single, new track, and using that track for the rest of the mix process, especially if you're squeezed for computer resources. Name the new track accordingly (e.g., "LeadVoc-PITCHED"). And as with comping, the original, now-unused tracks can be disabled/turned off to save processing and reduce clutter in the mix.

Here's a screenshot of the progression of tracks from original lead vocal, to comped lead vocal, to pitch-adjusted lead vocal (using Celemony's Melodyne), to a rendered version of the pitch-adjusted track. All mixing activities from this point forward will use this final track, not the original or any of the interim ones.

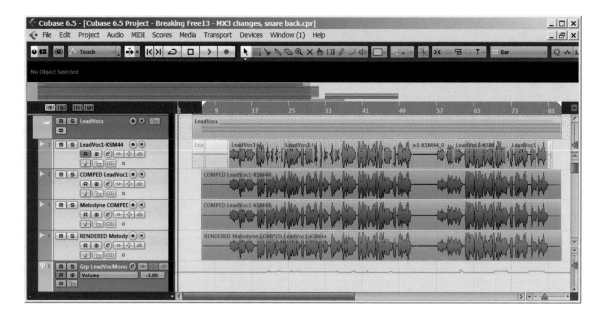

As a final step, we disable/de-activate all of the lead vocal tracks we're no longer using (shown darkened out in this screenshot), leaving only the final, rendered result active. This helps to keep us organized, and cuts down tremendously use of computer resources. But if we ever need to go back a few steps and change something, everything we need is available to us, and we only need to go back as far as the change dictates.

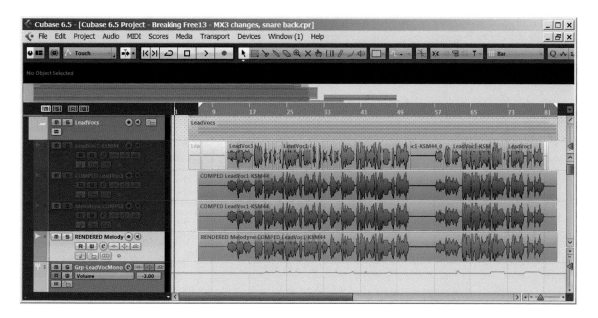

Cut down on clutter: put aside unused stuff

Here's one other thing you can do to "get your tracks in order," so to speak. Consider putting any tracks you don't actually use for the mix into an out-of-the way area in your project file (when I mix in Cubase, I put mine in a Cubase Folder called "Unused Stuff" at the very bottom of the track list). This area can include musical parts that have been ruled out, partial/unfinished tracks that never made it to the final cut, pre-comped/tuned tracks, etc. I much prefer this method to deleting them from the project entirely. The idea is to get them out of the way to cut down on clutter, but make them still accessible just in case you find yourself needing to access them later. If they're not already, you can disable or otherwise turn off these tracks so they don't use any computer resources while mixing.

And of course, do a "save as" when you're done with this cleanup process.

Initialize, set all tracks to nominal level

This step only makes sense if you haven't been building a mix over time in the same project file during tracking and overdubbing. If you've already got the basic layout of a mix that's evolved in an existing project file, then continue your mix from there. But if you're importing files into fresh tracks or just want to start afresh in "mix mode" with the tracks you've already got, then I recommend doing a "reset" or "initialize" of all settings on all tracks so you're starting with a clean slate. A reset will turn off all EQ, inserts, sends, panning, etc. and set the track's level to 0 dB (decibels).

Once you've initialized all tracks, in many cases you won't want to start mixing with all tracks' level set to 0 dB, because after you've adjusted relative levels between parts and added processing to them, chances are many tracks will end up too loud and cause digital clipping, on the individual tracks themselves and/or groups and/or the master bus. To avoid this potential problem, I usually start a mix with all tracks' levels set to the same nominal value, e.g., -10 dB. This provides me with enough "headroom" to work comfortably with all of the tracks in the mix and avoid having to fix troublesome distortion/overload problems later. With today's DAW software, it's fortunately very easy to set all of the tracks to the same nominal value with a single click, and not have to set them individually.

In the following screenshot, Cubase's "reset button" is the bright white, key-shaped icon on the far left, just above left of the tooltip that says "Reset Mixer/Reset Channels." As the tooltip implies, you can reset the entire mixer, or only selected channels. Note that the volume level on every channel is different before the reset.

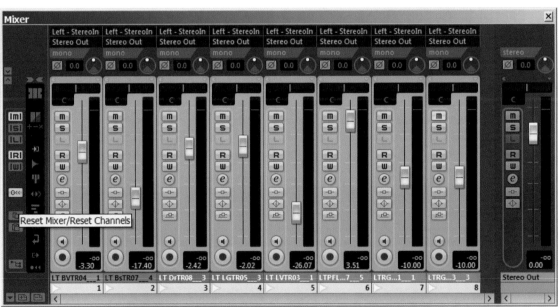

After we've reset the channels, all levels are set to 0 dB by default.

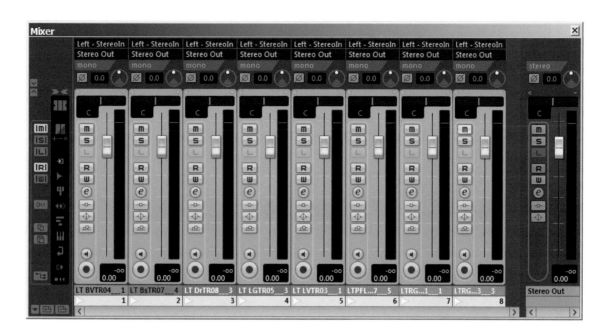

We still have one more step. The highlighted channels have been "linked" together in Cubase, and we set them all to a nominal volume level – in this case, -10 dB. This gives us an excellent point from which to start mixing, with plenty of headroom to work with without fear of overloading our channels (or the master bus) after processing is added.

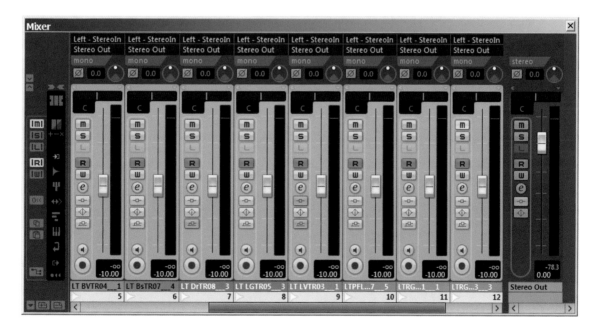

The reasoning behind setting all tracks to the same initial values is that it intentionally gives us a true picture of each track's relative musical "power" vis-à-vis the rest of the tracks in the mix. At this point, it's very easy to tell which parts of the mix were recorded very softly or very loudly and make initial adjustments, without artificial influence from different fader levels, EQ settings, compression, etc.

Assign initial virtual instruments

If you haven't done so already, at this point you'll want to assign any virtual instruments to MIDI tracks so that you can hear those parts as you're listening down to the initial tracks. You don't have to make final judgments about exactly which virtual instruments/patches you'll be using at this point; you just want something in the ballpark so you can get an idea of how the part(s) fit in a musical context.

In the following screenshot, we assign our "Keys1" MIDI track to a virtual instrument (in this case, Steinberg's HALion Sonic SE, and its "60s Drawbars Organ" patch). We've also co-located the virtual instrument's two associated mixer tracks ("HSSE Main" and "HALion Sonic") with the other "Keys1" audio, MIDI, and group tracks. If more than one MIDI track were to use this same instance of HALion Sonic SE, we wouldn't co-locate its tracks with a particular part. But in this case, we know that "Keys1" is the only part that's going to use this instance of HALion Sonic SE, so we can think of and manipulate all of the associated tracks together as a single entity.

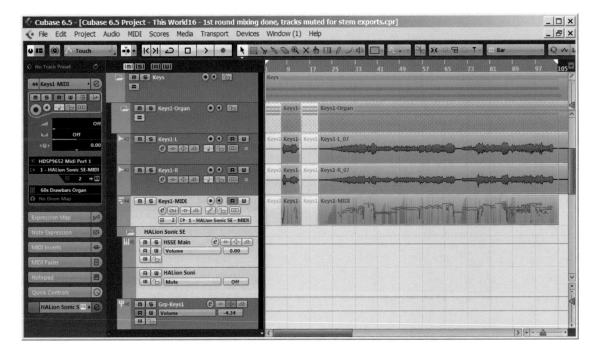

Here's a screenshot of the instance of HALion Sonic SE that's used by the "Keys1" part. You can see the associated instrument and patch assignments to the left of HALion Sonic SE.

Create initial time-based effects

As a final step in the setup phase of mixing, I like to go through the mechanics of setting up a few reverbs and/or delays – *that I may or may not use for the final mix*. Just because they're set up doesn't mean they have to be used later, but experience has shown me that they likely will, so why not get this left-brain activity out of the way with the rest of them? We may set up additional reverbs, delays, etc. as we go through the mixing process, but we'll start with these as a baseline.

I usually set up three initial reverbs for a mix: generally short, generally medium, and generally long. The subjective meaning of short, medium and long will depend entirely on the tempo, style, and general vibe of the song at hand. For an up-tempo, bouncy pop song, all three reverbs (even the "long" one) will have fairly short pre-delay and decay times. For a slow ballad, the opposite will be true. So you need to think in musical terms at this point and choose reverbs and delays that make sense within the context of the song at hand. Just so I have a relevant point of reference, I often use the snare and/or lead vocal track to feed the three reverbs to set their initial values. They might be adjusted again later during the mix process, but this is a good way to get them at least in the ballpark.

Here's a screenshot of the short, medium and long reverbs set up in a Cubase project.

41

An alternative to the "short, medium, long" approach to setting up initial reverbs is to set up reverbs that you expect to use for certain musical parts, such as lead vocal, snare and acoustic guitar. Either approach is fine; the concept of setting them up before you get started applies either way, so use whichever method works best for you.

Here's a screenshot of the alternative technique, using initial reverbs for snare, vocal and guitar.

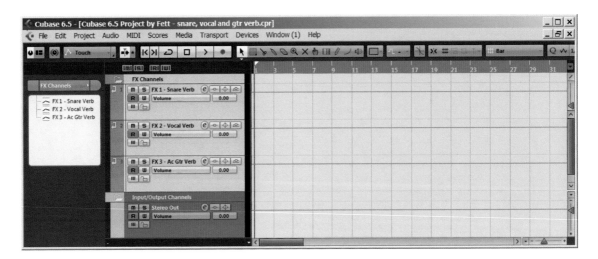

News flash! Presets are your best friend

Many of my clients ask me, "how do I know what reverb settings to start with?" My answer is invariably, "use presets!" I'm a huge fan of presets as starting points for any plug-in, not just reverbs. Why? Here's one of those "pro secrets" I discovered that's worth its weight in gold… When I was Technology Editor for a major music magazine for seven-and-a-half years, I attended at TON of music gear trade shows, like the NAMM and AES conventions. Over time, after watching countless software demos on the trade show floor, I realized that the software manufacturers were using their software's stock presets to show off their products' sounds. And then it hit me: *these companies put tons of work into making their presets sound as amazing as possible, because that's what the audience will hear when they demo their products.* Not only do they spend countless hours dialing in exactly the right settings on each preset, they also name them as precisely as possible so they can be sure they're pulling up the right presets during a demo. So if you have a compressor plug-in with a preset called "Killer Drum Overheads," chances are that preset has been developed using actual drum overhead tracks, and will be a pretty excellent starting point for yours. Sometimes, the presets are so good that they require no adjustment at all – even for your own tracks. Other times they might be a little too hyped and need some taming. But at a minimum, they'll get you quite a long way towards getting a really good starting sound.

Here are some examples of the preset lists from a couple of reverb plug-ins. The first is Steinberg's REVerence convolution reverb, which comes with Cubase. Because it's a convolution reverb, its presets are named to suggest the various sonic locations at which the reverb's impulse responses were captured.

This next example is from Universal Audio's UAD RealVerb-Pro. It's not a convolution reverb, and its preset names are more musical part-oriented (e.g., "Acoustic Guitar" and "Big Snare").

Another great use for presets, especially if you're a novice at using plug-ins or audio processing in general, is as an educational tool. Whenever I add a new plug-in to my arsenal, one of the first things I do is put the plug-in on a track and start scrolling – in real time while the track is playing – through the plug-in's presets. Not only does this process tell me what the different presets sound like (and how they differ from each other), it also allows me to compare the specific settings on each preset to see exactly how each parameter on the preset affects sound in general. If you'd like a crash course on how adjustments in different frequency ranges affect the tone of an instrument, or how the interaction of threshold and ratio affect how much compression is applied to a sound, simply crank up an EQ or compressor plug-in with a lot of presets, press Play, and start scrolling. You'll be amazed at the enlightenment you get from it, even if you've been doing this stuff for a while.

With this in mind, if you don't already have a starting point for your short, medium and long reverbs, try setting up three copies of the same reverb plug-in with "room," "stage" and "hall" presets. Or, if you're taking the part-specific approach to setting up your three initial reverbs (e.g., snare, vocal and guitar), try three copies of the same reverb with presets named "Bright Snare Chamber," "Dark Vocal Plate" and "Guitar Room Ambience" or similar, to match the mood of the song at hand. As with setting up virtual instruments, at this overall-listening stage of mixing, you don't have to get all of the reverb settings dialed in perfectly. Simply start with some stock presets, and make finer adjustments later in future phases.

Take a break, change headspace

Now it's time to take your first major break, and this is CRITCIAL. You've just spent quite a while in mechanical, technical, left-brain mode, manipulating a bunch of files, tracks, audio snippets, etc. If you've followed all of the steps above, you're pretty much done with left-brain activity for the purposes of the mix at hand, so it's time to take off that hat and put on your musical hat. It's time to think like a songwriter, musician and producer again. The only way to accomplish this is to take a break and let your mind rest before you embark on the right-brain part of the process.

Okay, if you haven't done so already, this is most definitely a time to do a "save as" and create a backup copy of your project files. Better yet, consider making your first backup copy on external media. You've done quite a bit of work so far, and it would be a shame to have to do any of it over in a worst-case scenario.

Phase 3: Core Mix (Virtual Sound Stage)

It's time to dig in and get musical. During this mixing phase, you're going to want to hear what you've got to work with in musical terms: what the parts are; when they play and don't play; and how the various tracks relate to one another in terms of their role in the overall conveyance of the song's message and feeling. This is the point at which you form a mental *musical* picture of where you want the mix to end up.

One very useful way I've found to do this is to think of the collection of instrumental and vocals parts being positioned on what I call a Virtual Sound Stage – a sonic representation of how you might hear an actual band performing on a live stage at a venue. If there are two guitarists, are they standing opposite one another on either side of the stage, or are they both off to one side, with the keyboards on the other side? Is the sound of the drums coming from directly behind the lead singer? Are the vocals very "out front" and in your face, or are they more blended in with the rest of the band? At a minimum, thinking about these kinds of questions will give you a basic framework for where to place things initially in the mixing process. Once you've got that down, of course, there are no rules: you can do anything you want. But at least the Virtual Sound Stage approach gives you a solid starting point.

Do "full up and dry" listen

Once I've gotten all of the preparation tasks out of the way in Phase 2, I like to start a mix by listening to all of the tracks at whatever nominal level I've set them to (see "Initialize, set all tracks to nominal level" in Phase 2), without any kind of processing at all – not even panning at this point. With the faders of all tracks at their nominal level, I close my eyes and simply listen intently to the "relative musical power" of each part against the others. I consider the following types of questions:

- Are the drums already way too loud and overpowering everything else? If so, they'll need to be turned down considerably at a minimum.
- Which instruments are playing very similar parts, and therefore potentially competing with each other for the same space, or muddying each other up a bit? They'll need to be made distinct and discernible from each other somehow, through some combination of level, panning, EQ and possibly effects.
- Where are the vocals "sitting" relative to the instruments? Perhaps they need to be brought forward from the outset to avoid being buried.
- How is the overall balance of low, mid, and high frequencies? Is there a nice "spread" there, with something occupying each wide frequency band, or are most of the tracks all bundled up around one narrow frequency area and competing for the tonal zone? If so, some radical EQ might be in order.

This is also the time to make initial, spot decisions on things you are *not* going to use in the mix, not just what you *are* going to use. Good producers and mix engineers know that less is more, and that just because a track was recorded, it doesn't mean it has go into the final mix. Don't be afraid to hit the "mute" button on tracks that just aren't working or just aren't needed and leave them muted, disabled and hidden in your "Unused Stuff" folder for the rest of the mixing process.

As I'm listening during this initial audition to all of the tracks "full up and dry," I'll take notes about my observations and what might need to change. Then, I go to work...

The 5 Primary Mixing Tools

There's a ton of stuff we can potentially do with a mix, but if you need to narrow things down and get a frame of reference to get started, this may help. When I mix, I envision that I have a "sonic arsenal" of five primary tools at my disposal:

1. Volume level
2. Panning
3. Time-based effects (e.g., reverb, delay)
4. EQ (equalization)
5. Compression/limiting

There are certainly many other tools and techniques available (e.g., non-time-based effects, layering, etc.) as well, but I view these five as my *primary*, go-to-first mixing tools. In very general terms, I consider each of these tools (and pretty much in the order listed) whenever I'm pondering what to do with a track or a musical part in a mix. We'll cover each of these tools in much more detail in following sections of this book.

Set initial relative levels

Before we start soloing things up and working in successive layers, we want to dial in a basic, overall balance of parts in our mix, based on the notes we took during our "full up and dry" listening step. The first, most basic weapon we have in our arsenal of mixing tools is *volume level*. In very general terms, if we turn up the level on a track, we'll hear more of it in the mix; if we turn its level down, we'll hear less of it. So if we're working with multiple tracks and want to balance them against each other, we'll want to start by turning up those that need to be louder, and turning down those that need to be softer. Relative levels alone do not make a mix, but they're the starting point that moves us towards getting the right overall balance between the musical parts. This is called "setting initial levels" and applies to both individual, non-grouped tracks and to group tracks.

To set initial levels on individual, non-grouped tracks (e.g., bass guitar), it's simply a matter of turning the track's fader up or down. For group tracks, it's a little more involved. The first thing we need to do is achieve a balance between all of the tracks that are being sent to the same group. For example, if we have neck and body tracks for a single acoustic guitar, we need to adjust those two tracks against each other to get the right general blend that we want for the guitar's overall sound. Once we've done that, then we can set the overall level of the guitar part using the group's track fader.

Often, the only three things I'll need to adjust on individual tracks that are being fed to the same group are level, minimal EQ, and panning. In the acoustic guitar example, I may set the level of the track for the body of the guitar slightly lower than the track for the neck of the guitar to balance the sound of the overall instrument or to make it less boomy. I much prefer this "automatic tone control" technique to using a lot of EQ on the body track to "dip out" this low end; in fact, this is one of the reasons why I would have used two mics to record the instrument in the first place. Next, if the two tracks are feeding a stereo group rather than a mono group, I will adjust the individual tracks' panning controls to position the instrument's different tracks within the stereo spectrum of the mix.

In the following screenshot from the Cubase mixer, the only changes to the two audio tracks for the acoustic guitar are slightly different levels and left-right panning. All other changes, including EQ, are made on their corresponding group track.

Here's a screenshot of the acoustic guitar's group channel settings, where the rest of the part's adjustments are made. In this case there's an inserted compressor (TC Electronic's PowerCoreCL) on the left, 2 bands of EQ adjustments in the middle, and a reverb send ("FX 2-SFX") on the right. On the far right, the volume of the part in the mix overall is set on the group track's fader.

49

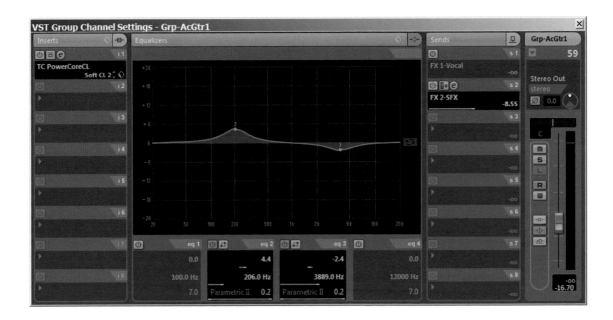

To recap, once the adjustments to the individual tracks that feed a group are made, I pretty much leave them alone and make most further adjustments (and add any processing) to only the group track, since it now represents the whole musical part. To balance the level of the acoustic guitar in the mix from this point forward, I'll use the acoustic guitar group's fader, not the individual tracks' faders.

Initial drum levels and groups

Note that, if there are drums in your mix, you're going to spend a fair amount of time working with the individual drum tracks and the group(s) to which they're assigned. The goal is twofold: 1) to get a good, realistic, natural balance between the various pieces of the drum kit; and 2) to get the sound of the kit "happening" in the overall context of the song. One of the most critical elements of achieving these goals is getting the right balance between close-miked pieces of the kit and the overhead and room mics. In general, the more overhead/room mics you have in the drum mix, the more "live" or "garage rock" it will sound, and the more close-miked elements you have in the drum mix, the more "close" or "tight" or "intimate" it will sound.

Because getting the right drum mix is so critical, I usually take full advantage of groups and use several just for the drums. While it varies from song to song, my typical setup is as follows:

- Kick In + Kick Out → Kick Group (mono)
- Snare Top + Snare Bottom → Snare Group (mono)
- Overhead Left + Overhead Right → Overhead Group (stereo)
- Tom Hi + Tom Mid + Tom Lo → Toms Group (stereo)
- Room Left + Room Right → Room Group (stereo)

50

- Hi-hat + Overhead Group + Room Group + Snare Group + Kick Group + Toms Group → Drums Group (stereo)

Here's a screenshot of the initial setup for a drum part's audio tracks and group tracks (12 audio tracks, 6 groups – my typical setup for drums). Note that there's no panning yet – only group assignments and basic level setting. Panning, EQ, compression and lots of other stuff comes later. This is just to get the drum part in the ballpark with the rest of the mix so far.

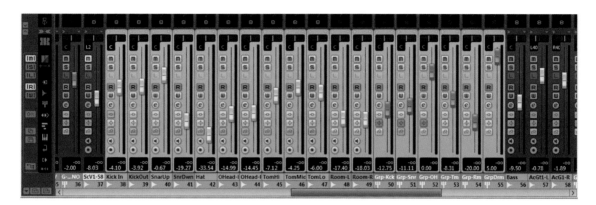

What I've found from using this setup is that, once I've got all of the individual pieces within each group adjusted correctly, I can make adjustments to the drums in the mix without having to jump through hoops. Less toms? No problem; just turn down the Toms Group fader. More "live?" No problem; just raise the Room Group fader, etc.

Note: In keeping with our we-don't-have-to-use-every-track-just-because-it's-there philosophy, although I may have 12 tracks of drums and their associated groups at my disposal, I might only end up using just a few of the tracks for my final mix. I've done plenty of mixes where I've only use a subset of the drum tracks and the muted the rest. I let the song and the purpose at hand dictate how many to use.

Hey, let's do a "save as!"

Set initial panning

After relative volume, the second weapon in our arsenal of mixing tools is *panning*. Note that I use the term "panning" here to generally mean placement within the *stereo* spectrum, although the concepts apply for surround-sound panning as well. There's a human psycho-acoustic phenomenon that works this way: as sound sources move away from the center and further out to the sides, our brains are able to "localize" them more. They become more distinct to us, even though their volume doesn't change. With panning, we take advantage of this psycho-acoustic phenomenon in a mix. So after setting initial, relative levels, the next logical step in giving parts their own "space" is to start positioning them between the edges of the stereo spectrum. Because parts become more distinct the further out they are, I tend to set a lot of tracks fairly far towards the extreme left and right in a mix, and leave less in the middle or the half-way points between the middle and the sides. One additional benefit is that, the more you take out of the middle, the more "room" you leave for the lead vocal there. Oftentimes, when volume and EQ and compression and effects just can't seem to make the vocal "pop" in a mix, the problem is that it's being too crowded by other elements that aren't panned far enough out of its way. In these cases, as you start to push things further to the left and right, voila! – the vocal suddenly takes center stage as intended, with no other adjustments.

Obviously, the Virtual Sound Stage concept can play a key role during this panning step, and help you decide where to pan parts to initially so there's some kind of logic to their placement. Typically, at least as a starting point, the kick drum, bass guitar, snare drum and lead vocal are all placed dead center, and everything else is a candidate for panning to the left and right. You may be wondering, "how can these four elements possibly all be placed in exactly the same spot and not get in each other's way?" Back to human psycho-acoustic phenomena: First, these four elements tend to have different dominant frequencies, so our ears are able to distinguish them by frequency range. Second, these four elements tend to play significantly different rhythmic roles in most music, and as a result, are usually performing different notes on different beats. Our ears are able to hear the four elements as four distinct sets of patterns, and our brains are able to tell them apart.

Beyond these four foundational parts being in the middle, pretty much anything goes in the world of panning. There really are no rules, so find what works for your mix and don't worry about how your panning "looks" in a logical sense, but rather, how it *sounds*. If you feel you've achieved a nice balance across the stereo spectrum once you've made your panning adjustments, then your panning is right for the song. Just keep in mind the general adage: the further out to the edges you push things, the more distinct they'll become to you – and the end listener.

Also keep in mind that different elements of a mix can move within the stereo spectrum during the course of a mix; they don't have to remain stationary. This movement can be used to great dramatic effect – or become really annoying, if not used well! But at this point, we're only concerned with setting the basic "anchor position" of each part within the stereo spectrum.

Drum orientation

Have you ever noticed that in some mixes, the drummer's high-to-low tom-tom fills travel from left to right across the stereo spectrum, while in other mixes, they travel from right to left? This positioning of the drum kit in a mix is a conscious thing called "drum orientation" and has two variations: *player* orientation and *audience* orientation. When you pan the various tracks of drums in a mix, you have a choice as to whether you want the drums to be panned as the drummer would hear them, positioned behind the kit looking out toward the audience from the stage, or as the audience would hear them, facing the stage. Either orientation is fine (some say American mixes tend to lean one way, and British mixes tend to lean the other way, but I've never bothered to do any research on the subject). The key is to be *consistent* with the orientation with *all of the drum tracks* in a mix. This is especially important with tracks that have been stereo miked (e.g., overheads or room mics). If you pan three mono, high-to-low tom tracks mid-left, mid-right, and far-right, for example, you need to make sure that the left and right overhead mics are not panned the opposite way, or the drum track will come out sounding really odd, and the listener will have a difficult time localizing the various parts of the drum kit.

In the following screenshot, we see that the individual mono audio tracks in the drum part are now panned to their respective locations in the stereo spectrum (indicated by the thin, blue, vertical lines at the top of each channel strip). Note that the audio tracks are the only tracks that are panned; the stereo group tracks to which their output is sent stay panned in the center. In this particular example, the drums are panned using drummer orientation, i.e., the hi-hat is on the left, and the toms are panned from left to right. It could have just as easily been done the other way around – as long as it's consistent.

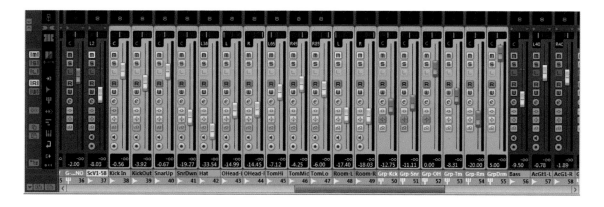

Good time to do a "save as."

Listen in context and adjust

Since panning allows us to hear specific parts more distinctly, after we've panned a bunch of parts in the mix, we'll likely have to go back and change some of their initial volume levels to compensate. In general, this means that we'll probably turn *down* a few things that are now further out to the sides, but that's not a hard-and-fast rule; let your ears drive your decisions here.

What part(s) to start with?

To this point, we've dealt with entirely "dry" tracks, free of EQ, compression, or any other sonic processing. That's because our purpose has been to lay a rock-solid foundation on which to build our mix. Now it's time to start getting creative! It's also time to start working on individual parts at a time. One of the most common questions I get from my students and consulting clients is, "what do I mix first?" When someone asks me, "do I start with the kick drum or the lead vocal?" my answer is usually, "yes!" The point here is that there is no absolute "right" way to structure or approach a mix. Having said that, there are a few conventions that, for good reason, have evolved over the decades that serve as excellent starting points. Some of the most common starting tracks are:

- Bass
- Kick drum
- Snare drum
- Lead vocal

The theory behind each of these is that you start with some kind of a "foundation" upon which you "build" the mix. In the case of bass (and partly, kick drum), you're starting with the lowest-frequencies and building the higher-frequency parts on top of them. In the case of kick or snare drum, you're starting with the most fundamentally rhythmically-oriented elements and adding chordal and melodic elements from there. In the case of the lead vocal, you're starting with the one element that will carry the message of the song the most (and potentially, the part that the listener will identify with first) and constructing a "supporting cast" around it. All of these approaches are totally valid, as are many more. So I recommend that people start either with whichever part(s) they're the most comfortable with, or whichever part(s) they think should take center stage or precedence over everything else. If you're just not sure, here's one approach/suggested order that you can use to get started:

1. Bass
2. Bass + Kick
3. Bass + Kick + Snare
4. Bass + Kick + Snare + rest of drum kit
5. Chordal "foundation" instruments: rhythm guitars, keys, etc.
6. Bass + Drums + chordal instruments
7. Color (character/flavor/fill) instruments: secondary guitars, keys, strings, fiddle, pedal steel, mandolin, banjo, etc.
8. Bass + Drums + chordal instruments + color instruments
9. Lead vocals
10. Bass + Drums + chordal instruments + color instruments + lead vocals
11. Background vocals

12. Bass + Drums + chordal instruments + color instruments + lead vocals + background vocals
13. Solo/feature instruments: lead guitars, fiddle, harmonica
14. Bass + Drums + chordal instruments + color instruments + lead vocals + background vocals + solo instruments

Note that with this approach, as you work on each successive part, it's critical to frequently listen to it in context with all of the parts that you've already worked on, to make sure that things are still holding together. If they're not, you'll want to adjust the current part before moving forward. If you don't, you'll end up spending a *lot* more time on the back end of the mixing process trying to make things fit retroactively.

Of course, as you finish each part/group, do a "save as" and a backup as appropriate.

Assign initial time-based insert/send effects

Time-based effects – especially reverb – are the next tool in our arsenal. Remember those three initial reverbs we set up during Phase 2? Well, now it's time to use them, at least skeletally. We'll be doing a lot of reverb assigning, adjusting, and creation throughout the course of the mix process, but first, it's good to set the reverb for a few key elements of the mix to initial values to dial in the overall vibe or mood of the song. For me, those key elements are usually the snare drum, the lead vocal, and possibly one primary chordal instrument (e.g., guitar or piano).

The snare drum is a phenomenally powerful element in most forms of Western popular music. It metaphorically *drives* the rest of the elements of the mix, laying down the rhythmic foundation for everything else to follow. It's one of the reasons that the snare is often the loudest or second-loudest element (after the lead vocal) in most mixes. The snare drum also happens to have an amazingly wide range of frequencies and volumes, and as a result, can be sculpted quite finely into just the right-sounding component to play its central role. One of the keys to dialing in the snare sound is to get it into the right "space" to set the vibe of the song, and one of the most important ways to do that is to give it the right reverb. That's why it's usually the first reverb that I assign and adjust in a mix.

Here's a snare-reverb-selecting procedure that has worked well for me: Start by soloing up the snare track and assign its first three send-effect slots to the short, medium, and long reverbs that we created in Phase 2. Turn on all three sends, with the send level for each all the way down. Now, as the song is playing, raise the send level for each reverb one at a time and listen to the "feel" that that particular reverb gives to the snare. What you're searching for is a reverb sound that both complements the musical *pattern* that the snare drum is playing at the song's tempo, and also enhances the song's *feel* that you're trying to convey in the mix, i.e., subjective terms like "snappy" or "dark" or "moody" or "fun" or "haunting." Assuming you set the initial parameters for the three reverbs in Phase 2 (even if you just used presets), you should be able to get pretty close to what you're looking for with one of the three reverbs. Don't worry too much about the *amount* of reverb at this point; just focus on the *feel* of the reverb.

Here's an example of one of the reverb presets from Steinberg's REVerence convolution reverb, called "Large Live Stage." Note that, although the picture implies that this preset might be ideal for acoustic guitar, there's nothing wrong with using on a snare drum – or any other part, for that matter. The only thing that matters is whether it *sounds* appropriate for the part within the context of the mix at hand.

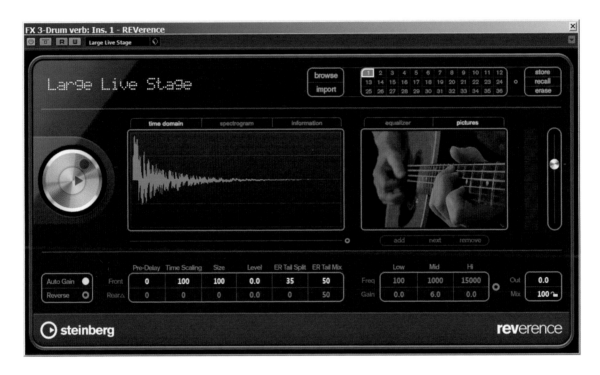

Note: on some occasions, you may actually decide that you like more than one of the reverbs at the same time. For example, you may like the sound of the shortest reverb for its "snappiness," and the tail of the longest reverb for "air" simultaneously. That's totally fine. You may experiment with two reverbs in series (one reverb feeds the other) vs. in parallel (both reverbs operate independently); there are all sorts of ways to get creative with reverbs here, and none of them is right or wrong. Use whatever works for the intent of your mix in faithfully conveying the message and feel of the song for the purpose at hand.

More commonly, you'll find that you like one reverb sound for the verses and a different one for the choruses and/or bridge (this is very typical if the snare switches between side stick and straight stick, or half time and double time, through the song). That's also fine; in fact, it's desirable, because it helps the mix ebb and flow as the song progresses. In this case, you'll probably want to create two separate instances of the snare reverb with slightly different settings, and switch between them using automation at the different sections of the song, rather than using just one reverb and switching its parameters back and forth, which takes more automation changes and more computer resources.

As you're going through this process of setting the fundamental snare ambience, you'll probably find yourself not only adjusting the send level of the snare track to the reverb(s), but also tweaking the parameters within the reverb(s) as well. This is the correct time to do it. You're setting up a fundamental element of the mix that you're going to build upon, so this is the time to take the time to get it right. After you've dialed in the right general reverb to use on the snare, you might also want to adjust that reverb's pre-delay to a value that matches the song's tempo, e.g., to an eighth beat. Some people simply do this by ear and get it in a ballpark that feels good musically; others use beats-per-minute-to-millisecond calculators to get the value mathematically exact. Some reverb plug-ins actually do it for you. Use whichever method works best for you; the point is to match the reverb rhythmically to the song.

As you're setting up the snare reverb(s), it's important to un-solo the snare track occasionally and listen to it in context with all the other tracks. This is the only way to determine the right *amount* of reverb on the snare track. It can't be done completely with the snare in isolation; it has to be done with all of the tracks playing together.

How to set initial reverb levels

My general guideline for setting any reverb send level is as follows: First, while listening in context with all tracks, raise the reverb send level of the track from all the way off to the point at which you definitely "notice" the reverb; then, *back the send level off a couple of decibels*. It's critical to make this final adjustment, or nine times out of ten, you'll end up with too much reverb, and the track will get washed out a little in the mix – especially if the mix gets a lot of compression later, which tends to bring reverbs forward and make them more noticeable overall.

After you've got the snare reverb set, go through the same process with the lead vocal. You may find that the snare and the lead vocal share the same reverb, or you may find that they use completely different reverbs. Both options are fine; whatever serves the mix for the purpose at hand is right. The important thing is to go through the process for both of them, and base decisions on the intended vibe of the song.

Reverbs and front-to-back positioning

Optionally, before you proceed to the next steps, you may want to set reverbs for one or more "foundation" chordal instruments such as acoustic guitar or piano. The main goal here, besides setting the vibe of the overall mix, is to "position" these elements more distinctly from front to back on the Virtual Sound Stage. This is an extreme generalization, but shorter reverbs (and shorter pre-delays on reverbs) tend to leave things more forward in the mix, while longer reverbs/pre-delays tend to push them back. Therefore, primary chordal instruments like guitars and pianos tend to have shorter reverbs (and/or reverb pre-delays) assigned to them, so that they sit more "out front" in the mix as featured instruments, and don't get washed into the background with everything else. But as with the snare and lead vocal, remember that a little reverb goes a long way!

Here's the same shot of the reverb we saw above, except that the reverb's pre-delay value has been changed from 0 to 4 (in the lower-left corner). This causes the illusion that the parts assigned to it are located slightly further back on the Virtual Sound Stage.

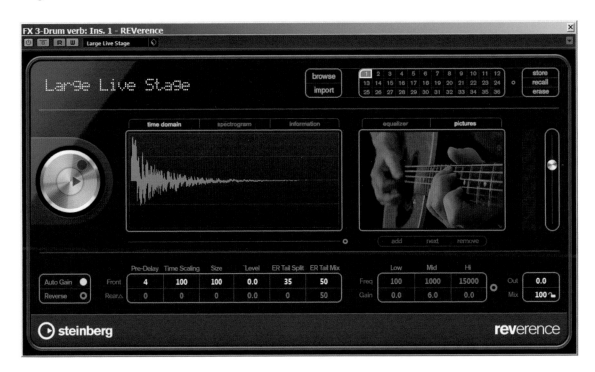

Here's another, more visual illustration of the impact of changing a reverb's pre-delay value. In this first screenshot (of the "Drums Short Snare" preset of Steinberg's RoomWorks reverb), the pre-delay value is set at 0 (just under the triangular-shaped graphic). This means that there is no delay between the time when sound arrives at the reverb and when the reverb kicks in.

In this second screenshot (of the "Drums Medium Snare" preset), the pre-delay value is set at 20. Note that the triangular-shaped graphic has moved over to the right, illustrating that the reverb kicks in later in time – 20 milliseconds later, in fact – creating the illusion that whatever is sent to the reverb is positioned further back on the Virtual Sound Stage than parts sent to reverbs with shorter pre-delay times (or not to any reverbs at all).

By this point, you may have four or five different reverbs in your mix, even if you haven't used them all yet.

Do an incremental "save as" as you finish setting up reverb for each part/group.

Set initial EQ

Now that we've achieved a basic balance with levels and panning, and established the central "vibe" of the mix with some reverbs, it's time to start developing the unique "tonal character" of each instrumental and vocal part. The order in which we do this is fairly arbitrary, but I've found that setting each part's EQ, then compression, then other insert effects, then send effects (besides those initial reverbs already set in the step above) works pretty smoothly for me.

EQ is probably one of the least understood and under-appreciated weapons in the mixing arsenal. Many times, inexperienced mixers will reach for a volume fader on a track when they should really be reaching for the EQ knobs. EQ *is* actually a volume control; it works by raising or lowering the *level of particular frequencies*. For example, sometimes the best way to "bring up" an electric guitar is to simply give it a little "bite" at 3 kHz and leave the volume of the rest of its frequencies right where they are.

Having said this, I also believe that, if a track is well-recorded with the right microphone(s) (and more importantly, right mic placement), front-end preamp(s) and processing, you may not need to EQ it at all. The time to EQ is either a) when a part needs tonal distinction and/or correction to help place it in the mix against other parts, or b) when a part needs obvious differentiation as an *effect*, to make a bold statement in the mix (e.g., the "telephone" sound on a lead vocal). The first form of EQ is generally more subtle; the second is generally more extreme.

Finding the "tonal essence" of a part

If I do decide that a particular part needs tonal distinction, I use an EQ-setting method that I like to call "finding the tonal essence" of the part. By "tonal essence," I mean that frequency (or set of frequencies) where the part naturally "sings" or resonates. Due to their very nature, instruments and voices have certain dominant frequencies that are very much a part of their character. You might have seen a chart that shows the primary frequency ranges of all of the common orchestral instruments and where they overlap. These combinations of frequency ranges play a huge part in our ability to tell the difference between a tuba and a clarinet just by listening to them. But within these broader frequency ranges, each individual instrument also has its own, unique resonant frequencies that distinguish it from all other instruments of the same type. That's a key reason why two acoustic guitars – even of the exact same make and model – sound different from each other. The same applies to individual human voices. When we use the EQ-setting technique of "finding the tonal essence" of a part, we're dialing in those narrower ranges of "character" frequencies on each instrument and voice, and emphasizing them in the mix on purpose. We might also lower certain "problem" frequencies on a given part to de-emphasize them.

Additive vs. subtractive EQ

Before we talk about that, though, we have to mention "additive" EQ vs. "subtractive" EQ. There are two things you can do with the level control on an EQ frequency: raise it or lower (in geek speak, "attenuate") it. In the audio engineering community, there's a contingent of people who subscribe to the "never increase EQ, only decrease it" philosophy. This approach, called "subtractive" EQ, is based partially on the fact that, especially with analog gear, when you turn up the volume at any frequency, you are turning up any *noise* that exists at that frequency as well, and noise is generally a bad thing in a mix. For example, if you turn up 60 Hz (cycles) on an electric guitar track to give it more bottom end, you will also be turning up any electrical hum from the amp and/or pickups that was recorded along with it. The same idea applies to noisy microphones, preamps, console channels, etc. So what's the alternative? In our electric guitar example, proponents of subtractive EQ would suggest simply turning down other frequencies outside of the 60 Hz range to achieve the same result; you get more sound at 60 Hz without adding any noise.

This philosophy definitely has merits, and there are other aspects/benefits to it, but if you've got carefully-recorded tracks that haven't gone through a lot of noisy analog gear and/or tape, I feel you can be just as effective with additive EQ (i.e., mostly turning up frequencies you want to emphasize). I also find that subtractive EQ takes more time and is a little trickier to do well. In practicality, I end up using a combination of EQ approaches; I'll generally use additive EQ for bringing out the "tonal essence" frequencies, and subtractive EQ for reducing overly-dominant frequencies (e.g., extreme boominess in acoustic guitar at 300-or-so Hz) or fixing technical problems (e.g., 60-cycle hum in electric guitar). When using subtractive EQ to fix problems, I try to use notch filters or parametric EQ's with an extremely narrow frequency width, or "Q" so that I only affect the problem frequencies and don't take away any of the "good" character frequencies that are nearby.

All this to say that, if you look at one of my mixes, you're probably more likely to see boosted frequencies on tracks than you are to see cut frequencies. It just happens to work out that way for me, but more for practical reasons than deliberate or philosophical ones.

The following screenshot shows a combination of additive and subtractive EQ. On this hi-hat track, much of the low end has been "rolled off" (decreased, using subtractive EQ) to essentially eliminate rumble and low-frequency parts of the drum kit (toms and kick) that might have bled into the hi-hat mic during recording. Conversely, just under 8 kHz – evidently, a key frequency for this particular hi-hat in this particular mix – has been boosted considerably (by 8.5 dB) using additive EQ.

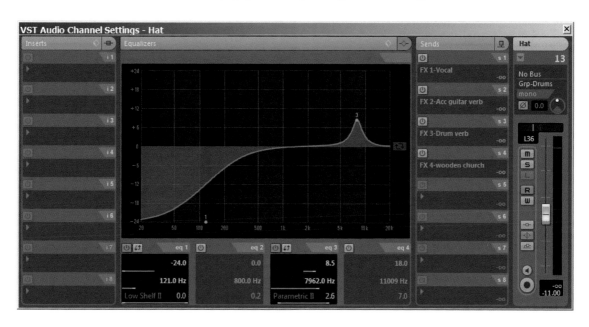

This next example shows the use of mostly subtractive EQ. This stereo group of drum overheads has two frequencies that have been "dipped out" considerably, while there is a slight rise in the frequencies at the top end.

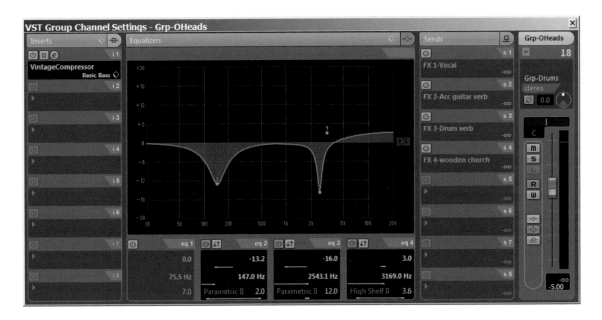

Here's an example showing a combination of very subtle subtractive and additive EQ on an acoustic guitar part: a couple of dB boost at just under 200 Hz to add a little warmth, and a slight dip at just under 7.5 kHz to tame a little bit of string rattle or other brightness.

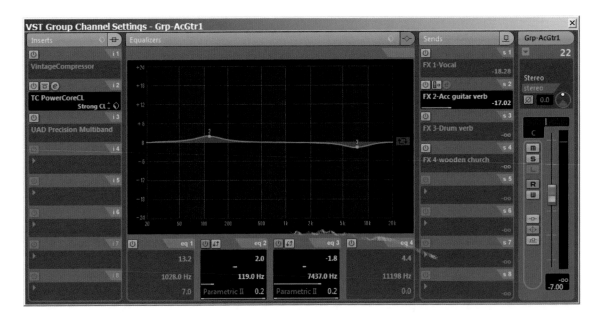

Here's one more example, this time using strictly additive EQ. Evidently, the "Loung Lizard chorused Rhoades" [sic] preset from a virtual instrument needed some significant "help" at two midrange frequencies to place it in the correct tonal context vis-à-vis the other parts in this particular mix.

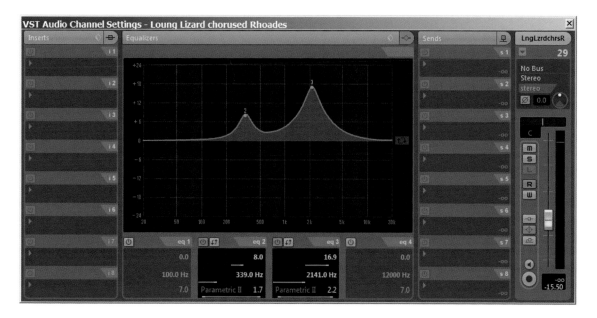

EQ sweeping

So, how exactly do we "find the tonal essence" of a part? Through a process I call "EQ sweeping." First, I start by soloing the part, and then picking an arbitrary frequency band (e.g., the second, or lower-mid band on a 4-band parametric EQ) and raising that band's level control artificially high (at least 10 dB, perhaps even more). This extremely high level is temporary; it won't end up there, but it ensures that I'll be able clearly hear the effect of my actions as I go through the process.

This screenshot shows the second band of the EQ being set arbitrarily high while sweeping through the frequency spectrum in search of this part's "tonal essence."

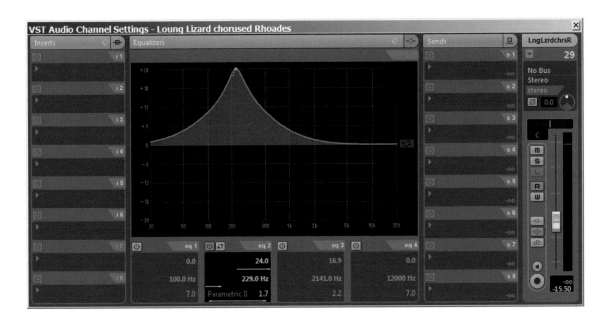

Next, as I listen to the part in solo, I'll move the frequency band control back and forth between lowest (left) and highest (right) frequencies until I hear a frequency area that sounds really good to me in terms of the tonal character of the instrument or voice. This may sound kind of like voodoo, but trust me, once you've done this a few times, you'll get pretty quick at hearing those "magic" frequencies that really bring out the best tonal elements of a part.

Once I've got that first "special" frequency in the ballpark, I'll sweep back and forth a little more, in tiny increments, until I have it dialed in just right. At that point, I've got the right overall frequency band setting.

Next, I'll continue to listen to the soloed track and vary the "Q" (frequency band width) control back and forth between narrowest and widest until I find the narrowest frequency range at which that "special" frequency is still brought out, and surrounding frequencies aren't emphasized too much. At this point, I've really pinpointed a very specific, unique "character zone" for the part.

Finally, I back off the frequency level control and bring it down to the lowest possible point that the character zone is still audible, but doesn't overpower the part's other frequencies. After all, I still want the instrument or voice to sound "natural" and "real," unless I'm going for some extreme, over-the-top, oddball sound, which at this point in the process, is usually not the case.

This screenshot illustrates how, after we've found a "tonal essence" frequency, we bring the frequency band's level down to a much lower point.

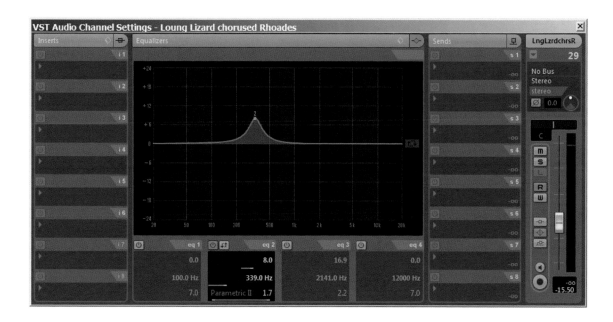

At this point, I may be done, or I may decide to dial in one or more other "tonal essence" frequencies on the same part. Sometimes, for certain instruments, such as snare drum, kick drum and bass guitar, or the human voice, a combination of two frequencies is ideal. But keep in mind that, the more frequencies you emphasize on a track in this way, the more chances you have of other tracks competing for those same frequencies, and you may end up having to re-adjust a lot later to compensate for the conflicts. So if one frequency will do the job, it will make your job much easier later in the mixing process.

For fixing problem frequencies (like boom, mud, knock, hum, buzz and hiss), I use exactly the same turning-it-up technique to *find* them, but then *lower* the frequency's level (i.e., to a negative value) at the end of the process. In this case, I'm using subtractive EQ for correction.

This screenshot shows that, after finding problem frequencies by initially boosting to an arbitrary level so I can zero in on them, I then tame them by attenuating the frequency I've identified.

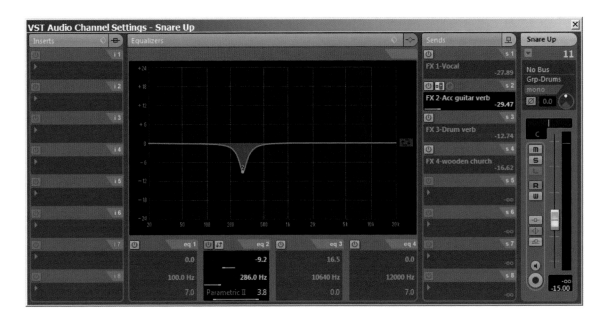

This may sound like an awful lot of work, but it's really not. Dialing in the "tonal essence" of a part can take a few minutes, but sometimes it can take as little as 30 seconds, especially after you've gotten familiar with the process and inherently know which frequencies typically work for which instruments and voices. While there are always minor variations from song to song, many of the EQ settings on the same part will be very similar from mix to mix in a single project, especially if you use the same setup (mic, instrument, player, studio, preamp, etc.) when you record different parts.

EQ spreading/splitting

When we use the technique of bringing out the "tonal essence" of each part effectively, each part will end up having an EQ curve that looks different from all other tracks' EQ curves. The end result is that each part "owns" a unique set of frequencies in the mix that no other part matches exactly, so that each part has its own little "character stamp" or "EQ zone" that it occupies and nothing else is competing for. I call this "EQ spreading" (or EQ splitting) among the parts in a mix, and it can be your most powerful tool for making each part distinct and discernible among a potentially complex combination of instruments and voices. Chances are that by this point you'll also have carved out a nice, even distribution of sounds across the entire frequency spectrum of low, mid and high frequencies.

EQ flipping/swapping

But what do you do when you have two parts that share essentially the same "tonal essence" frequencies, e.g., doubled electric rhythm guitars that play basically the same part with the exact same setup? At a minimum, you'll probably want to pan them away from each other in the stereo spectrum. And you might use different effects on each one, but that still might not be enough to make them distinct from one another in the mix. At this point, you're going to want to employ another technique I call "EQ flipping" (or EQ swapping). This technique involves taking two different frequencies and setting them exactly the opposite way between two similar parts, the result being that each part "owns" only one of those two frequencies, and "stays out of the way" of the other frequency. So, in the electric guitar example, on the first guitar, we'll boost one frequency – let's say +3 dB at 4 kHz, and cut another frequency – let's say -3 dB at 2 kHz. Then, on the second guitar, we'll do the opposite: cut by -3 dB at 4 kHz; and boost by +3 dB at 2 kHz. When the two guitars are played back together, suddenly they're more distinguishable from one another.

Note that the frequencies (4 kHz and 2 kHz in our example above) can even be fairly arbitrary. Within reason, it's less about which two specific frequencies you pick than it is about making the boosts and cuts shared between them enough to make them sound different from each other.

The following two screenshots illustrate the EQ flipping technique with two guitars. In this particular mix, electric guitar 1 ("EGtr1") has a boost at about 200 Hz and a corresponding cut at about 1,400 Hz. Conversely, electric guitar 2 ("EGtr2") has the exact opposite: a cut at about 200 Hz and a boost at about 1,400 Hz. The end result is that each guitar "owns" a particular frequency zone in the mix. Note that they are also panned hard left and right opposite each other, which further helps them to "stay out of each other's way."

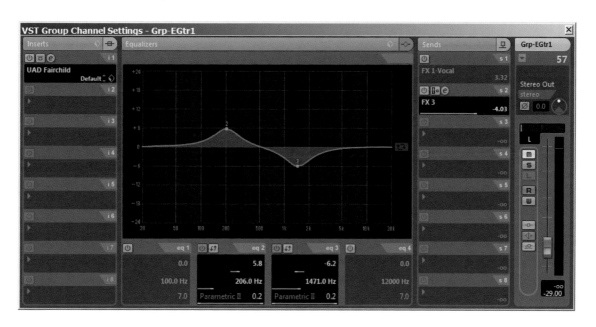

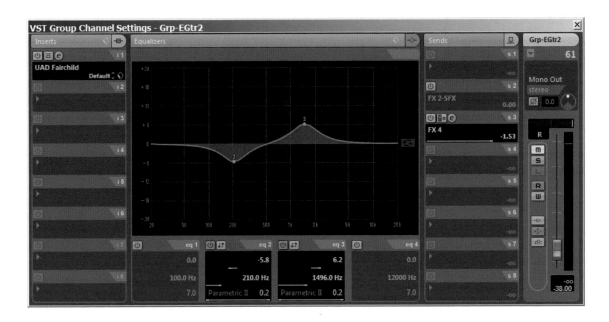

The two guitar parts might even sound a bit odd when soloed up individually, but the *blend* of the two accomplishes the result. This is a good illustration of the art of *balancing* different components in a mix; it's much less about how they sound by themselves (which the end listener will never hear) than about how they blend together as a whole.

Listen in context and adjust

With every one of the EQ techniques I've described above, it's important to frequently un-solo what you're working on and listen to it in the context of the overall mix. If not, you'll find that a part that might sound killer soloed up is suddenly really overpowering (even when turned down) or just sounds completely outside the overall sonic "palette" of the mix. Just as when setting reverbs, you'll most likely find yourself backing off a dB or two with some of your EQ settings once you hear them in context with other parts. That's a normal part of the process, and should be expected.

Once you've got your EQ dialed in on your various parts, it's likely that, just as you had to do after panning, you'll need to go back and re-adjust levels to compensate for the increases and decreases in volume at the various parts' frequencies.

Set initial compression

After I've spent a fair amount of time dialing in EQ settings, I reach for the next weapon in the mixing arsenal: *compression*. Note that you'll often hear the terms "compression" and "limiting" being used together. Limiting is simply compression with a very high ratio – they work exactly the same way. As with EQ, if a track doesn't need to be compressed, then I don't apply compression to it. But often, especially in today's environment, in addition to the overall mix, most if not all parts in a mix have some amount of compression applied to them. The goal is to use compression to *enhance* the parts and *add impact* to them, not simply to slam everything as much as possible. One of the most common things I hear in amateur mixes is compression that is over-used to the point that it actually ends up having the opposite of its intended purpose, and things sound squashed, lifeless, and indistinct.

For reasons I don't really understand, compression seems to be one thing that may new recordists are most "afraid" of, and there are a lot of misperceptions about compression. The first misperception is that compression automatically makes things louder, and the more compression you use, the louder things become. In reality, compression *reduces* the dynamic range of audio material, and actually makes it less loud overall. However, in doing so, it enables us to raise its overall volume after the fact. It's that after-the-fact part that brings louder volume – not the compression itself.

Compression threshold

The next misperception I hear a lot is that compression ratio (e.g., 2:1 or 10:1) is the most important value in compression, and the higher the ratio, the more compression you'll have. Not so! One of the first types of questions many of my consulting clients as ask me is, "what compression ratio should I use on bass guitar (or some other part)?" And my response is always, "how loud is the bass (or other part) to begin with?" The reason I ask this question is that the most fundamental value in compression is *threshold*, not ratio. The threshold does two things: it determines whether there's any compression at all; and it determines how often compression happens. So until you set the threshold correctly, none of the other values – attack, release, knee, ratio, etc. – are going to matter much. The purpose of the threshold is to determine *at what level of volume the compressor kicks in*, and therefore, how much of the incoming material will be compressed at all. So if you have very loud material and you set the threshold at -20 dB, you might be compressing nearly everything all of the time because the volume of all of the material is above the threshold. On the other hand, if you have very soft material and you set the threshold at the very same -20 dB, you might never have any compression, because the volume of all of the material is below the threshold.

Just to be clear, the *lower* the threshold, the *more* material will be compressed. Or to put it another way, threshold is one of those values that, the lower you set it, more impact it has. That's because everything that *exceeds* the threshold is what is compressed, and everything below it is left alone.

The following screenshots show how significantly the threshold setting can affect how much material is compressed – regardless of the ratio setting. In both of the following two examples, the ratio remains at 3.76:1. In the first example, the threshold is set at -14.6 dB, while in the second example, the threshold is set at -38.6 dB. The graphic on the right side of the compressor shows how much of the incoming material will be compressed and by how much, based on all of the compressor's values. In basic terms, the graphic shows that, with a relatively high threshold of -14.6, the amount of material that's compressed will be fairly small – just a little bit at the top of the loudest portions of the material. Conversely, with a relatively low threshold of -38.6, a significant amount of the incoming material will be compressed.

Following on with our example, in the following screenshot, the threshold remains at -38.6, while the compression *ratio* is lowered from 3.76:1 to 2.18:1 (i.e., less compression). Even with a lower *degree* of compression, more compression will take place overall than in our very first screenshot above, because more of the incoming material will exceed the threshold.

By the way, there are a zillion designs (and user interfaces) for compressors out there, so you might encounter a compressor that doesn't have any components labeled "threshold." In these cases, either the threshold is pre-set and you can't change it, or more likely, there's an "input gain" (or similarly-named) control that allows you to raise or lower the volume of the signal coming into the compressor. *Raising* the input gain control accomplishes equivalent of *lowering* the threshold level; i.e., the higher the input gain, the more material that will be compressed. Some compressors have both input gain and threshold controls, giving you a lot of flexibility (and possibly, more potential for overwhelm!).

Here's a screenshot of a popular compressor plug-in that, just like its hardware cousin, has no threshold control: the UAD 1176SE from Universal Audio. In this case, the equivalent of "threshold" is set by the INPUT control on the far left.

Based on the explanation above, the very first thing you should do when setting up compression on a part is to set the threshold. You can start with a fairly arbitrary compression ratio – let's say somewhere between 2.5:1 and 6:1 just so you can actually hear the effect of the compression when it happens. And you can start with a fairly arbitrary medium value for attack and release. You'll adjust these values later, after you've got the threshold in the right place. Or, as I've mentioned before, you can start with a preset if this all seems too daunting right now.

First, as with EQ sweeping, while you're listening to the track in solo mode, raise and lower the compression threshold until you find the spot where you hear the compression kicking in often enough to actually be processing the material. Now you've got the right general ballpark. Then, if you intend to have a fairly limited dynamic range on the part in the mix (an electric rhythm guitar part, perhaps), then lower the threshold a little more, so that you're compressing a fair amount of the time. On the other hand, if you intend to have a more natural, open dynamic range on the part in the mix (a fingerpicked acoustic guitar, perhaps), then raise the threshold up just a little bit so that more of the material isn't compressed than is. Obviously, you've got to be thinking about each part in terms of its overall role in the mix at this point, to know what you're going for. I nearly always set my threshold by ear and not by numbers; in fact, I'll often close my eyes when I do it, so that I know I'm relying totally on what I'm hearing and nothing else.

Compression ratio

Once you've got the threshold set, you can increase or decrease the compression ratio to determine *to what degree* the compression is applied whenever the compressor is active. This is where you're setting how much you hear the effect of the compressor on the compressed material. As with threshold, I tend to set compression ratio using my ears, not my eyes or specific numbers. Regardless of the specific values, if it *sounds* right, it *is* right. I've compressed different parts at ratios from 1.1:1 to Infinity:1, depending on the material at hand. There really is no right and wrong here, but the one thing I do try to avoid is "hearing" the compression more than I "hear" the material itself – like pumping and other artifacts – that distract from the *musicality* of the part.

Compression attack and release

Once I've set the threshold and ratio, I make adjustments to attack and release, which totally vary by what the part is playing. In general terms, I want a fast attack and release on things that happen quickly, such as snare hits in an up-tempo song, and a slow attack and release on things that happen slowly, such as whole notes on a bass guitar on a slow ballad. This is an extreme simplification (after all, that's why compressors offer a range of fast and slow values for attack and release), but it's a good place to start.

When I set attack and release on a specific part, I'm listening for two main things. With attack, I want to make sure that the initial, transient sound at the beginning of notes or beats isn't cut off too quickly. Nothing will kill the energy of a snare drum part like a compressor attack that is set too fast. I listen (in solo) and adjust the attack until I can hear that initial, transient sound come through fully, and then I leave it alone. On the release side, I want the tail end of things to be compressed long enough so that they sound even, and don't suddenly change dynamics in the middle. So on a bass guitar part, I want to make sure that the longest notes that are being compressed stay compressed until they finish; otherwise, I'll need to increase the release value.

Other aspects of compression

This is not a tutorial on all aspects of compression. There are many compressor designs out there, and many compressors offer numerous other values that can be adjusted, such as knee (which determines how smoothly the compressor kicks in and out, using a curve) and make-up gain (which allows you to turn up the volume of the material before it ever leaves the compressor – very handy); but threshold, ratio, and attack/release – in that order – are the most important to get right first. If you focus on them, chances are you'll be on your way to really good use of compression in your mixes.

One more thing about compression: compressors, like any gear, do not all sound the same. They're based on different designs with different intentions. So whatever you do, take the time to try different *types* of compressors on the various parts in your mix, not just different values on the same compressor. Oftentimes, what a track really needs is a totally different-sounding compressor, not a lower threshold or higher ratio. Especially with so many excellent (and different-sounding) compressor plug-ins available, it has never been easier to experiment and learn.

Let's back up a few levels and remember *why* we're setting compression at this point in the mix process. Just as with initial level, panning and EQ, we're working on a) getting a good *balance* between parts; and b) bringing out the *unique character* of each individual part. We can use compression to get too-extreme swings in a part's volume under control, and also to enhance or emphasize the "energy" of the part. With these guidelines, I'll typically look for things that need a little taming with compression and make basic settings there, and then I'll go to work on "energizing" certain parts. To me, anything is a candidate for compression, but generally, I only compress when I feel it's needed for those two guiding purposes. When I compress too many parts, or compress too extremely, I find that my mix starts to reach a point of diminishing returns and just gets deader and deader. When that happens, it's time to go back and let off on some of my compression to allow things to breathe again. Nothing will take the life out of a mix faster than over-compression.

Having said all this, here are some guidelines that you may find useful as a starting point for approaching compression in a mix. But please don't take them as gospel; I've kind of settled into this general approach after years of mixing, but I probably still "violate" it almost as often as I follow it:

- More up-tempo generally calls for a greater degree of compression to complement the "up" energy level of the song

- Vocals can really be hurt by over-compression; I'd much rather "ride the fader" (with automation) on a vocal track in combination with compression than use compression alone to get a vocal track's vocal dynamics under control
- If recorded well, acoustic guitars generally require minimal compression and can sound *really* unnatural when over-compressed (one of the most common signs of amateur mixing). Ditto for acoustic piano.
- Overdriven electric guitars seem to *love* to be compressed for "crunch" (my secret weapon: UAD Fairchild)
- Bass guitar can benefit from compression for *sustain*
- Snare drum can really "pop" well when compressed effectively (and by a fair amount)
- Kick drums can be fattened up quite nicely with correct (and pretty extreme) compression
- Compressing drum overheads and/or room mics can really add to the "liveness" of a track
- "Orchestral" parts (like strings) and organs can get really washed out when compressed too much

Obviously, there's plenty more to compression than this, but it should give you plenty to work with for starters.

Listen in context and adjust

As is the case with EQ, as you're setting compression values, it's important to un-solo a particular part you're working on, listen to it in context, and then make adjustments accordingly so it still fits into the overall vibe of your mix. And you'll likely need to re-adjust track levels as well, since compression's main impact is on the dynamic range (i.e., the range of *volume*) of tracks.

Create and assign effects for specific parts

Time for a little review... So far, we've used the following tools in our mixing arsenal:

- Volume level
- Panning
- Initial time-based effects
- EQ
- Compression

Now it's time to dig a little deeper into effects. The word "effects" covers an enormous array of possible sound manipulation, from time-based effects like reverb, delay, flanging and chorusing to overdrive/distortion, tremolo and rotary speaker simulation, as well as a lot of new, "other-worldly" effects that are being introduced every day. But I group them together in our arsenal because I think of them as all having a similar role: to provide uniqueness – a very specific-sounding "voice" – to a part within a mix. And because of their uniqueness, it's often the effects that are used in a mix that give it its unique "sonic stamp" beyond just the basic arrangement and choice of instruments and voices. We've already done some effect-setting with our initial reverbs; now let's do some more.

Insert effects vs. send effects

You may already be aware of the differences between what are referred to as "insert effects" and "send effects," but just in case you aren't, for the purposes of mixing, it's quite simple: "Insert" effects are used only on a single track (an audio track, MIDI track, group track, etc.). They are placed in-line on the track; i.e., they are "inserted" into the track's signal flow (hence the name). "Send" effects, on the other hand, can be shared among multiple tracks, and their output is the sum total of all of the different tracks that share them. In order to make this work, each track "sends" its output to an effect that's located on a separate track of its own (not inline) and combines all of the sending tracks' outputs together. Importantly, the output of the send effect is not returned to the individual tracks; instead, it is routed independently to another part of the mix, most typically the stereo master.

A send effect, since it's not set up in-line on any of the tracks that use it, needs to be instantiated somewhere in the mix. In the DAW world, it is instantiated in an "aux effects track" or something similarly-named. Regardless of what it's called, it's a single instance of the effect that is then "pointed to" by the send-effect slots of each of the tracks that share it. This effects "summing" or "bus" design is consistent with the way analog consoles and outboard effects work, so if you've ever worked with hardware-based gear, there's nothing new to learn here.

The following screenshot shows the insert and send effects slots on a lead vocal track in a Cubase project. On the left are eight *insert* effects slots, labeled "i1" through "i8." In this particular example, there are two insert effects assigned: a DeEsser and a Multiband Compressor on slots i2 and i3. On the right are eight *send* effects slots, labeled "s1" through "s8." There is a single send effect assigned: a vocal reverb in slot s1.

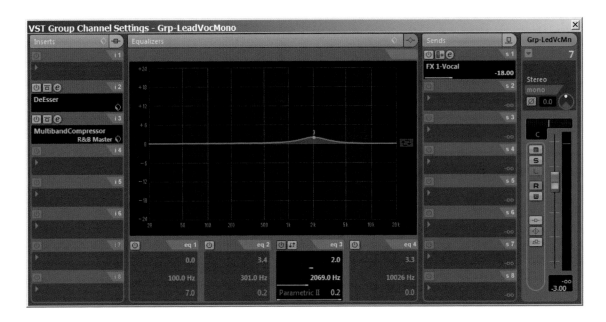

A side note: You may notice that the lettering of the last two insert effects slots, i7 and i8, is a different color than the lettering on the other six. That's because slots i1 through i6 are "pre-fader," meaning that the track's volume fader has no impact on the level going into them. The last two slots are "post fader," which means that the track's volume fader increases or decreases the level going into them as it is turned up or down. All of the send effect slots, on the other hand, can be either pre- or post-fader, depending on how their pre/post switch is toggled (it's the little icon just above the "1" in "FX 1-Vocal" in slot s1 in the screenshot above). There are many potential reasons for setting an effect slot either pre- and post-fader, such as gain staging (for signals that are too loud or too soft going into an effect slot and need to be controlled) to creative effects like turning a track's volume level all the way down but still hearing only the "wet," effected signal from a pre-fader reverb send.

When to use insert vs. send

With today's DAWs and effects plug-in designs, virtually any effect can be used as either an insert or a send effect, so which way to go? A general rule to follow is this: if you might end up sharing an effect between multiple parts (e.g., a reverb), set it up as a send effect; if you only expect to use an effect for one part (e.g., an auto-wah on a guitar solo), set it up as in insert effect. There are certainly variations to this rule, but it works most of the time. It will also save you precious computer resources in your mix: you could set up the exact same reverb as an insert effect on five different tracks rather than as a single send effect, but that would require five times the memory and processing power to accomplish the exact same result.

We've already talked about setting the overall, time-based send effects of reverb and delay. While they certainly contribute to the "sonic stamp" of a mix, so far at least, we've used them more for placement of parts in the mix, from closer up to farther away. The other time-based effects – particularly chorus and flange – play more of role of defining "character" than of distance placement. These effects, along with the others mentioned above, are also often (though certainly not exclusively) used as insert effects rather than send effects.

By this point in the mix process, you've got every track/part pretty much dialed in in terms of where it's going to "sit" in the mix. Now, with effects, you can add that one final layer of unique identity to the individual parts to round out the final sound. Less than using effects to fix problems or balance things against each other, we're carving out a unique personality for every instrument and voice on our Virtual Sound Stage. This is the point, for example, at which I'll add specific delays to electric guitars to make them "bigger", or chorusing to bass and backing vocals to make them "thicker," or a 60-millisecond delay panned opposite an organ part to give it more "depth." The focus at this point is entirely subjective and musical. This when you want to get as creative as necessary, possibly even "break" some "rules" and come up with something fresh, unique, and musically compelling. So take some time with this step, and have fun with it. Try scrolling through a bunch of effects plug-ins' presets, just to hear what they do. You might land on something really interesting.

Note: while I'm obviously a big fan of using presets on individual effects plug-ins, I'm not as hot on DAW manufacturers' "track presets," where a whole bunch of plug-ins are strung together as insert and/or send effects on a single track. While they may show off a bunch of the manufacturers' available plug-ins, they can be overdone, and use a ton of computer resources in the process. I recommend checking them out in your environment and then deciding whether they work for you.

Having said that, here's a screenshot of a track preset for bass guitar that comes with Cubase. This particular preset includes a combination of some very specific, 4-band EQ, and two insert effects: compression (VSTDynamics) and chorus.

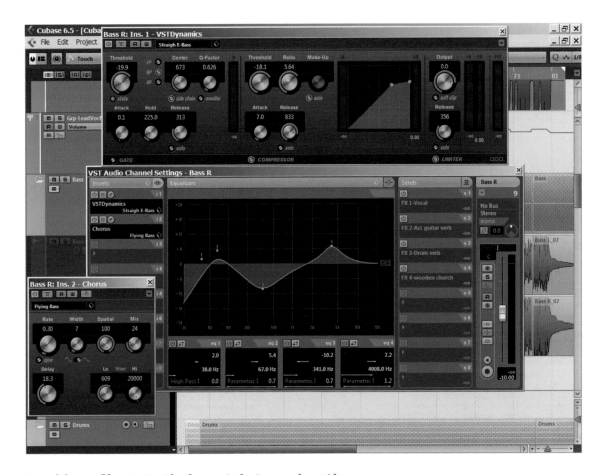

Matching effects to their parts' stereo locations

Here's another one of those pro secrets that can really help to keep your mix from getting muddied up by effects: When using an effect (especially reverb) on a track that is panned, pan the effect to the same location in the stereo spectrum. For example, if you have a guitar part that's panned to middle-left, rather than leaving its stereo reverb set to its default of panning equally wide left and right, set the stereo reverb to pan the middle-left as well. This will accomplish two things: first, it will help to localize, or "anchor," the guitar part on the Virtual Sound Stage by locating everything to do with the part in the same stereo position in the mix; and second, it will cut down on what I call "ghosting," where there are effects from a part in places on the Virtual Sound Stage where the part isn't actually present. It's better to place other parts' reverbs in those locations where *they* reside, so that the mix doesn't become one huge jumble of washed-out reverb. Of course, there are no rules here, and sometimes you might specifically want to spread a part out across the stereo spectrum (as in the 60-millisecond organ delay example above), but just be aware that setting all of your effects to a default of equally wide left and right has the potential to make them all wash into each other and make individual parts stand out less distinctly.

The screenshot below shows how three effects channels (FX 3, FX 4 and FX 5) are panned to match the panning of three corresponding guitars that feed them. This helps to localize each guitar part and "anchor" it positionally in the stereo spectrum.

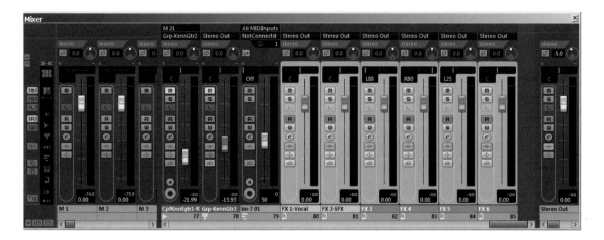

One potential downside to matching effects' panning to the parts that use them is that, if you have many parts panned to many locations, then you're going to need to have separate instances of each effect that is panned, rather than sharing effects among multiple parts. For example, if you have three guitars in three different stereo locations that each use the exact same reverb *settings*, you still have to instantiate three separate copies of the same reverb plug-in, because each one will be panned to a different location. This can eat up scarce computer resources pretty quickly.

Set initial automation for basic control

At this point, you've been listening to all of the parts in the mix long enough to notice tracks that need some significant raising or lowering of level in spots because of the way they were recorded. This would be a good time to insert a few rough volume automation moves to get these spots under control. You'll probably have to refine this basic automation later once you've made other changes, but putting these moves in now will at least get you pretty close. You could have done some of this basic control-type automation earlier, but I recommend waiting until this point, after you've made a number of other changes that potentially affect a track's variation in volume levels – not the least of which is compression.

In the following example, the hi-hat track has been raised in volume in a couple of sections where the drummer played a pattern very softly. It needs to come up in these sections in order to be heard evenly with the rest of the drum track, and the mix overall. We use volume automation to accomplish the task.

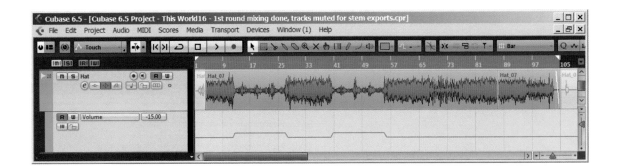

Conversely, sometimes a snare drum part needs to be "tamed" when it switches from side stick to full stick (typically between verses and choruses, respectively). The following screenshot shows how we do that with volume automation. It's also a good illustration of why we group similar tracks together and make changes to the group instead of the individual audio tracks. In this case, we only have to automate in one place – the Snare group track – instead of on both the Snare Up and Snare Down audio tracks.

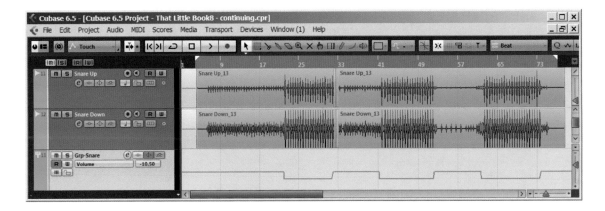

And of course, do a "save as," etc.

Take a break, change headspace

Once we've reached this point, our mix should be sounding pretty darn close to where we want it to be. From here on out, it's mostly a matter of repeating some of the steps we've already taken and tweaking things. But before we do that, just as we took a break after the left-brain setup of our mix in Phase 2, it's time to take another break so we can rest our ears and give ourselves a chance to back up many levels and listen to our mix more from the "big picture" perspective.

Phase 4: Iterative Adjustment and Automation

If we've done our previous steps carefully, this phase should be an almost entirely "fun" part of mixing, where we spend most of our time enjoying our masterpiece as we tweak it. And since we've taken a break and have fresh ears (and a fresh head), we should be able to sit back and spend more time listening than we do adjusting. In fact, one of the strongest recommendations I can make is to try to do a lot of the listening part this phase *with your eyes closed*. For those of you who just can't resist watching waveforms go by on the screen as you listen, then I recommend literally turning off your computer monitor so you don't have a choice!

Re-balance parts

During this phase, you're listening to (and hopefully, liking!) the mix as a whole and looking for two primary things:

1. Parts that are buried
2. Parts that stick out too much

At this stage in the mix process, when we close our eyes and listen, we should be able to pick out each individual part *if we consciously focus on it*. If we can't "find" a part in the mix when we try to, then it's getting buried, and we want to iteratively go back through our arsenal of mixing tools – in possibly the same order that we initially used them – and see if tweaking each one brings the part up to the point where we can "find" it on cue. Perhaps just turning a fader up a little is all we need. Or maybe we need to pan a part out a little further to the side, or even to the opposite side from where it is now. And so on down the line of mixing tools until we find the right one(s) to make it sit right in the mix.

For parts that stick out too much, we can use the same tools to "tame" them. Of course, if parts only stick out too much in certain places, it might be a simple case of automating their level in those places and leaving everything else alone. This leads me to the next part of this mixing phase...

Re-consider arrangement and flow (and adjust accordingly)

In addition to making subtle tweaks to individual parts' sounds to balance them, this is the time to think again of the mix as a *progression* of a story or a *journey* of sound. We want the mix to "breathe" and move, and take the listener on a bit of a ride to keep them interested. We do that by having things *change* as the mix progresses. When you start thinking this way, in terms of sections of the song, you can view the sections as separate, standalone mixes that are all based on the same mix "template," but can vary on their own. You've done all the hardest work in developing the template; now you can reap the rewards by letting each section make its own statement with very few changes. At this point, you'll make possibly heavy use of automation, but for the purposes of ebb and flow rather than simple control. Some of the things that we have at our disposal to change during the progression of a mix are:

- When a part plays and doesn't (mutes)
- Changes in level
- Panning movement
- Tonal changes (EQ)
- Switching between effects
- Changing individual effects' parameters

You'll potentially automate not only bi-state, on/off stuff, but also *gradual* changes like raising and lowering effect send levels.

When a part participates (or not)

There's nothing that says, just because an instrument was recorded from the downbeat of the song to the last note, it has to remain in the mix for the entire course of the song. Here are some examples:

- Perhaps the piano can start the song by itself.
- Perhaps the electric guitars should only come in at the second verse, to "up the energy level" compared to the first verse and chorus.
- Perhaps the organ should only be present in the choruses, to give them a different "texture" from the rest of the song.
- Perhaps the bridge should be a breakdown that only features the drums, bass and one acoustic guitar.

ANY part that's been recorded is a candidate for coming and going in the mix. This is where your arranging and production chops (rather than your technical, engineering finesse) have a chance to shine.

In the following screenshot, it's been decided that the Dobro part will not play in certain sections of the song, so that part has been silenced accordingly, using mute automation (the mute automation track is shown at the bottom, beneath the audio and group tracks).

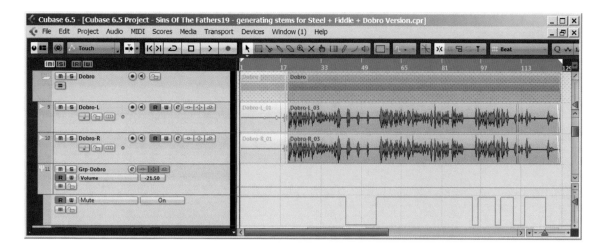

The tone of a part

Just because a piano part has a "mellow" sound in the verses doesn't mean it can't have a little more "edge" in the choruses to add to their intensity in the context of the song. With today's amazing automation tools, it's really easy to switch the EQ settings on a track (and back again) at any moment in a mix. So why not bump up the upper mids on the piano in the choruses? Of course, when you do this, you might have to bump back the mids on something else in the choruses so they don't muddy each other up, or you might need to temporarily lower the level of the piano to compensate, but you get the idea.

A tried-and-true technique with tonal variation in many forms of popular music is making the lead vocal brighter in the choruses and darker in the verses. This technique not only gives the song an ebb and flow, but also subconsciously reminds the listener that the choruses are more "significant" than the verses, for lack of a better term. Another variation on this technique is to switch between "natural" EQ and "effect" EQ in different sections of the song, the most typical example being the "telephone voice" EQ (in general, boosting all frequencies somewhere between 1 kHz and 4 kHz, and cutting all the rest). This technique has been used a lot because, when used effectively, it can "grab" the listener's attention at just the right moments.

This screenshot shows one example of the classic "telephone voice" EQ.

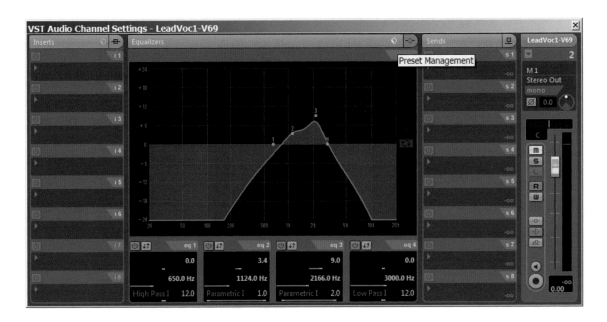

Anything is a candidate for a change in EQ at different sections of the song. For snare parts that use side stick in some sections and straight stick in others, I very frequently use two different EQs – one to emphasize the "wood block" aspects of the side stick, and another to emphasize the "snap" and/or "box" sounds of the full snare drum.

Here's a screenshot of a snare drum track, showing a change in EQ between the side stick and full stick sections of the song.

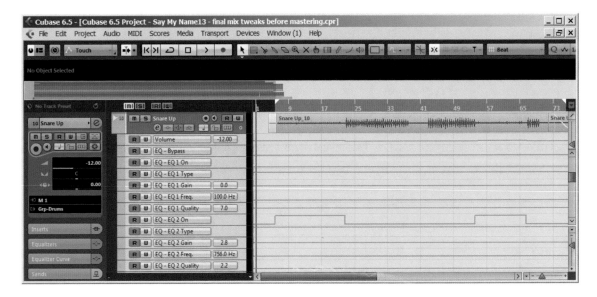

Positioning a part

Movement of a part through a mix can take many forms. Sometimes, it's literally *moving* within the stereo spectrum. A subtle movement of a vocal from one position to another over the course of a section of the song can be the perfect tool for differentiation between sections, and setup for subsequent sections that follow. Or a quick, bouncing pan from side to side between words in a lyric or parts of a guitar solo can really help to emphasize them. Of course, like any sonic tools, real-time panning can be overdone, but when used with subtlety and finesse, it can take the listener on quite a satisfying ride.

The following screenshot shows extensive use of a combination of panning and volume automation in background vocals through the course of a mix.

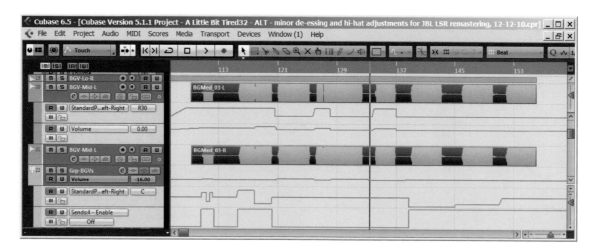

Another tool for changing the positioning of a part during the course of a mix is reverb and delay. As discussed earlier, longer delay times (including reverb pre-delay) and decay times generally push things to the back of the front-to-back continuum and make them seem further away. So if you want to "feature" different instruments or vocals in different sections of the song, in addition to simply changing their volume, you can change their reverbs' pre-delay and decay times to move them forward and backward. And as with any of these changes, if you move one thing up or back in a section, you may need to move something else in the opposite direction in that section to compensate, so that they don't end up crowding each other.

When to say "chuck it!"

One of the things you may find after working with a mix for quite a while is that, at a certain point, regardless of what adjustments you make – even having parts coming in and out – it still sounds cluttered. At that point, it's time to seriously consider whether certain parts need to be removed entirely. This is when you test your true objectivity as a creative person! The question to ask yourself is, "which is ultimately more important to me – serving the song and the end listener, or saving parts that I might have spent hours or days creating and recording?" Only you can decide, but one of the best traits of a great producer is knowing when to take things out as much as when to put them in. If you want to see this in action in the most perfect way, listen to any of the mega-zillion-selling records that Quincy Jones produced for Michael

Jackson. There's really never all that much going on in terms of instrumentation or layers of tracks, which means that the focus is never stolen from Michael Jackson's lead vocal. There is no finer illustration of "less is more" than that.

Of course, do a "save as" and a backup here.

Take a break, change headspace

Okay, we've listened, tweaked, listened some more, tweaked again, and possibly chopped the mix into several "mini-mixes" that vary considerably from one another. That's a lot of brain work, so it's time to take another break to hit the reset button on our creative engine before we proceed to the final stages of mixing.

Phase 5: Master Bus Processing and Tweaks

Alright! We've made it to the home stretch. For all intents and purposes, from a musical standpoint, our mix is pretty much done at this point, especially if we've gone through all of the previous steps carefully and methodically. But it's still not "in the can" quite yet – there's still more we can do to make our masterpiece even better. In order to do this final step right, we have to *really* change our mindset. In particular, instead of focusing on individual tracks, groups, or even musical parts, we need to back up quite a bit and focus only on the mix as a *cohesive whole*. I call this the "hundred-foot level," at which we try as much as possible to experience the mix the same way the end listener will: as the song in its entirety, in a stereo recording.

That means we have to avoid the temptation to go back and arbitrarily tweak things on an individual track or part level. While we will make minor, track-level adjustments based on our listening (otherwise, why would be bother listening?), most of our activities will be focused on the stereo master track (also referred to as the "master bus"). We want to try to make lower-level tweaks only when absolutely necessary to *fix problems*; if we don't, we'll end up second-guessing a lot of decisions we've already made (and a lot of work!) and potentially waste a lot of time, and in the extreme, make our mix sound worse, not better.

Here's a screenshot of the stereo master bus channel in Cubase. You'll notice it has eight insert effect slots on the left, just like other channels, but there are no send effect slots. That's because the master bus is the logical "end of the line" as far as audio signal flow within the mixer goes. From this point, it's directly out to audio hardware and/or a file – there's no other place inside the mixer to "send" the audio from here.

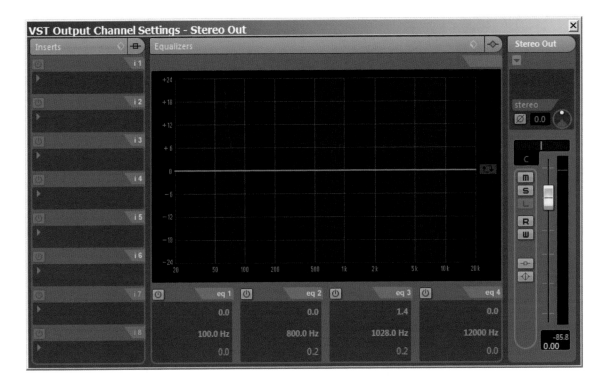

Master bus processing vs. mastering

At this point, you might be thinking, "isn't this really *mastering* we're talking about?" Well, yes and no. While we might be thinking like a mastering engineer to some degree by listening to the mix as a whole entity, we're not trying to squeeze every last nuance of volume and "commerciality" out of the mix, or consider it in the context of other songs that may share the same musical project. *That* is part of what mastering engineers do. Instead, we're trying to maximize *this particular mix's message and musical vibe*, unto itself, without consideration for other songs' mixes or the final stages of commercialization.

Don't touch that dial!

In order to stay on task and think at the hundred-foot level, I recommend – even before we've got things dialed in on the master bus – that a significant part of this phase be done *with the computer monitor turned off*, our eyes closed, and a pad of paper in our hands. This helps us to avoid interrupting our thinking, constantly shifting between the one-foot level and the hundred-foot level (or worse, between right and left brain), and making quick changes out of context. Even if you're fortunate enough to be mixing on a console or a control surface that has physical knobs and faders, for much of this phase, you should pretend it's not there and not touch it prematurely.

Proper listening levels

So, here's how it works… Bring up the last version of the mix project in your DAW and turn off the computer monitor. Position yourself in your "sweet spot" (your mixing position where you hear things the most accurately). Make sure the output volume of your monitor speakers is somewhere in the 60- to 80-dB (decibel) range. If you don't know how loud your speakers are, you need to either invest in a basic decibel meter (inexpensive and available at electronics stores like Radio Shack), or download at least one of the zillions of smartphone/tablet decibel meter apps that are available online (many of them for free). If you decide to go the app route, since they can vary wildly in their measurements, I strongly recommend downloading several, and calculating an average reading between them all, and/or reading the apps' user comments and focus on the one(s) that users praise for their accuracy.

Regardless of how you measure and set your speaker levels, I don't recommend listening at volumes louder than about 85 dB, except for extremely short time periods, to spot-check things. Not only will listening at safe volumes help to preserve your hearing (without which, you couldn't mix at all), it will also yield you better mixes. Why? Mostly because of an acoustic phenomenon called the Fletcher-Munson Curves, which basically reflect the fact that the amount of various frequencies we perceive changes with volume, and the higher the volume gets, the more skewed our hearing becomes. For example, as we turn up the volume on a rock mix, we *think* we hear the bass as it actually is, but in reality, we perceive more of it than is there. So what's the result when we listen to the mix later at a lower volume, where our ears are more accurate across the entire frequency spectrum? It lacks low end and sounds completely thin – especially for the genre.

It's pretty common for most people that the longer they mix without taking breaks, the more they tend to turn up the volume of their speakers, so make a point of checking your volume levels throughout the mixing process. If you find you've cranked the volume control on your speakers a lot since a couple of hours prior, it's time to take a break and rest your ears. If you leave the volume knob at the same position before you leave the room, you'll be amazed at how loud (too loud) it sounds when you come back to continue the mix. So keep your volume in check, both to protect your long-term hearing and to guarantee yourself better mixes.

Crank it *down*!

In addition to not listening louder than about 85 dB, I also recommend periodically listening to a mix at intentionally very low volume. Many people never think of doing this, since it's not typically how end-listeners will hear the music, but it's a great way to identify things that unnaturally stick out in a mix (or don't stick out the way they're supposed to). For a band mix, in very general terms, I listen for three primary things to be clearly audible above everything else at very low volume: the lead vocal, the snare drum, and the bass guitar, in that order. If these three elements are clearly there and I can still hear the rest of the "track" at a reasonable level behind them, I've got a pretty good idea that I'm in the right ballpark. If, on the other hand, I notice the backing vocals or the guitar solo really stand out above the other elements at low volume, chances are they're too loud. Or if I can't hear the bass, it probably needs to be goosed up a little.

Please leave the room...

A variation on this low-volume technique is to listen to the mix from a different room than where the monitor speakers are located. Turn the monitors up to the level at which you normally listen, start playing back the mix, and step into the next room, leaving the door open. You should generally be able to discern the key elements in the same way from the other room that you do when listening at low volumes right in front of the speakers. This version gives you an added perspective on the same goal.

Master bus mixing approaches

If you've consulted other resources about mixing, you might be wondering why we're waiting until this seemingly late stage to add any processing to the master bus. Many mixing engineers put processing on the master bus (typically a compressor-limiter) as the very first step in mixing, before they do anything else. They do this for multiple reasons, two key ones being that they deliberately want the sound of the master bus processing to influence their decisions as they mix, and they want to be closer to a real-world scenario, since the master bus will be processed at some point anyway.

I call this style of mixing "mixing to the master bus." There's absolutely nothing wrong with that approach, and I've certainly mixed some projects that way myself. But over time, I've found that if I defer master bus processing and get my mix sounding as good as I possibly can without it, then when I do apply it, it takes my mix to an even higher level than if I'd done it the other way around. It's similar to the concept that if you mix on speakers, your mix will sound killer on ear buds, but not necessarily the other way around.

Another reason I wait until the end to apply master bus processing is that, in some cases, it just isn't needed. The mix may sound just fine the way it is, or if I know the mix is going to be mastered by me or someone else, I'll defer that kind of processing until mastering. You're welcome to use whichever approach works best for you, but the discussion here assumes that the mix is essentially done before master bus processing comes into play.

Master bus processors

Once you've consolidated all of your notes after listening, you should have a list of a few things you need to do to the master bus. Some of the tools you're going to use on the master bus are the same ones you used on individual tracks while mixing: primarily EQ, compression/limiting, and on occasion, effects. Many DAWs come with (and many third parties also offer) plug-ins specifically referred to as "master bus processors" and you might want to start with one or more of those to address your list of issues and carve out the tone of the overall mix, and give it punch, presence, and good spatial placement. These "master bus processors" come in many flavors, and are usually some combination of EQ, compression/limiting, time-based effects, and "exciters" or "finalizers." Many of these exact same plug-ins are also used in mastering, and are fine to use here on your master bus, but just be careful not to over-apply them – especially if you intend to have the mix mastered after the fact, whether by you or someone else. If your mix is overly-hyped and "maxed out" as the result of the over-use of this type of processing, there won't be any room to do much else in mastering. And just as with plug-ins on individual tracks and groups, if you're not really sure where to start with master bus processing, I recommend starting with master bus plug-ins' presets. Listen carefully as you scroll through them, choose whichever preset sounds best on your mix, and tweak from there. If you don't have any master bus-specific plug-ins, you can use any EQ, compression/limiting, and other plug-ins that you used on individual tracks and groups on your master bus.

The following two screenshots show an example of using a processor on the master bus – in this case, a UAD Precision Limiter from Universal Audio – in addition to some very slight EQ in the midrange. Note that the limiter is on slot i7, so it's post-fader, meaning that if we raise or lower the master bus's volume fader, it will affect the level of the signal going into the limiter.

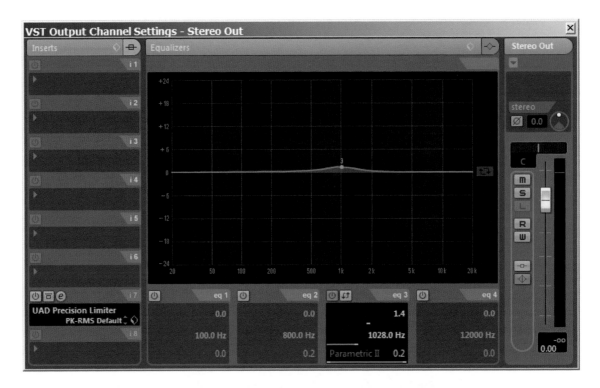

Check/adjust master bus level

One other critical thing you're going to want to do at this stage is to make absolutely sure that you're not overloading the master bus with too much volume. This can happen at three different places:

1) At the output of tracks or groups that cause the total input to the master bus to exceed 0 dB;
2) At the output of any processing that's been inserted on master bus (such as the plug-ins mentioned above) that causes the total output of the master bus to exceed 0 dB; and
3) At the output of the master bus itself, where it exceeds 0 dB before its signal is sent to audio hardware and/or rendered to a stereo file.

Keep in mind that, because of the architecture of modern DAWs and extremely high-resolution audio formats, individual tracks' and groups' levels themselves can go well over 0 dB with no problems; there's plenty of "headroom" to handle the numbers that are generated. So if you suddenly see the meters on a track or group jumping up to +5 dB, don't worry unless the total output of all tracks and groups is causing the input to the master bus to exceed 0 dB. Unlike individual tracks and groups, if the level of the master bus exceeds 0 dB, *you are guaranteed to lose data*. At that point, there's digital distortion in the mix, so it needs to be fixed before the final mix is rendered.

Here are a couple of examples of master bus processors that are being overloaded by too much volume from the master bus fader. In both cases, the extreme presence of the color red in the meters is telling us that something is drastically wrong with the level somewhere!

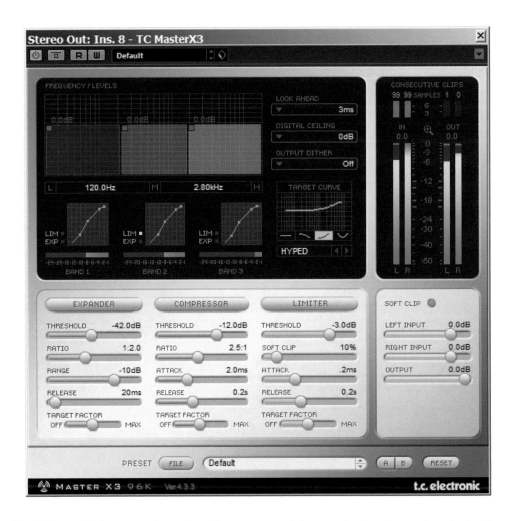

If you've followed the practice of setting reasonable nominal volume levels in Phase 2 and kept an eye on individual tracks' and groups' outputs throughout the mixing process, chances are that the first instance in the list above won't occur, or not by much. If there are only a few peaks that cause the input to the master bus to exceed 0 dB momentarily, then a little simple "fader riding" with automation in just those spots on the original tracks/groups can fix the problem. You can also use a "brick wall" style limiter on those tracks to tame those occasional peaks.

If the problem is more constant, then we'll need to turn down the master bus fader so that its output to any inserted post-fader plug-ins doesn't exceed 0 dB. The place to find out if this is happening is in the inserted plug-ins themselves. Most "master bus processor" plug-ins have meters for both input and output. Keep lowering the master bus fader until the input at the master bus plug-in(s) no longer exceeds 0 dB. At that point, the output of the inserted post-fader plug-in(s) becomes your final level control, so make sure to check the plug-ins' output meters, and if they're exceeding 0 dB, turn them down as necessary.

Note that this approach assumes that the master bus processing you are using is inserted post-fader and not pre-fader. Some DAWs give you the option of inserting master bus plug-ins either way. In Cubase, for example, the master bus has eight inserts; the first six are pre-fader and the final two are post-fader. I place my master bus processing on those last two inserts, so that I can control the input to them simply by raising and lowering the master bus fader. If I was to use the six pre-fader inserts instead, changing the master fader volume would have no effect on their input. In that case, I would have to turn down all of the tracks in the mix to avoid overloading the inserted plug-ins.

Here's an example of two master bus processors on the two post-fader inserts on the master bus: a UAD Cambridge EQ and a UAD Precision Limiter. Since they're post-fader, they'll be affected by the master bus's volume fader. Note that in this example, the order is EQ, then limiter. It could just as easily have been limiter, then EQ, depending on what kind of sound is desired.

Set initial master bus EQ

Setting EQ on the master bus is generally a subtler process than setting EQ on a track or a group. That's because, instead of using EQ to "bring out the tonal essence of a part," we use EQ on the master bus to sculpt the overall tone of the mix and/or fix minor tonal problems we might have heard when listening to the mix at the 100-foot level. So we're generally talking about 1- or 2-dB boosts or cuts of EQ in a couple of frequency ranges. The kinds of things you'll be addressing with EQ here are whether the overall mix needs a little more "air" on the top end, a little more "warmth" (or less "mud") in the low-mids, some "presence" (or less "harshness") in the "vocal" midrange, or a little boost on the bottom end for power. You can use the same kind of EQ you use on a track or group, or a "master bus EQ" plug-in that's tailored for this specific function, or a finalizer/exciter plug-in (which, among other things, works typically on frequency-related information). Just be careful not to overdo it – especially with a finalizer/exciter plug-in – if the mix is going to be mastered as well.

If the mix doesn't need any "help" with frequencies (and it's very possible it doesn't, if you've followed all of the steps so far), then there's no need to do any EQ processing on the master bus.

Here's a closer-up screen shot of that UAD Cambridge EQ. You can use your DAW's internal, "stock" EQ on the master bus, an inserted EQ plug-in, or a combination of both.

Set initial master bus compression/limiting

It's more likely that you'll have some kind of compression and/or limiting on the master bus than EQ. But just as with EQ, the degree of compression/limiting you use on the master bus will likely be significantly less than you would use on a track or group. You should be thinking more in terms of compression "adding polish" or "gluing the mix together" rather than trying to make the guitars more aggressive or getting the vocal to "pop." Today's mixes tend to use far more compression and limiting than in the past, so it might be appropriate to push the amount of compression here, but be careful not to over-push it and end up sucking the life out of all the hard work you've done on the mix. Remember that the music still needs to breathe a little to have maximum emotional impact, even with a lot of compression/limiting. This is a balancing act that you'll get better at the more you do it.

As with EQ, you can use any kind of compressor and/or limiter that you'd use on a track or group, or a more specialized "master bus compressor" on the master bus. There are some really outstanding master bus compressors available today, and many of them have the specific purpose of approximating the "analog warmth" of the master bus on traditional mixing consoles. Some of them are even based on specific analog console models. When used well, these plug-ins can add some real "magic" to your mix, both smoothing it out and pulling it all together at the same time. Tape emulation plug-ins, though more subtle than compressor/limiters, are also good for this purpose.

Here's a screenshot of a typical plug-in that emulates analog tape saturation: the Yamaha Vintage Open Deck. This kind of plug-in is often used on the master bus to provide a final, analog-sounding "warmth" or "smoothness" to the overall sound of a mix.

Compression, limiting, or both?

Master bus processing can involve just compression, but more often than not, both compression and limiting are used. The compression is there to add punch, presence, warmth and the like, and then limiting is used to control any remaining peaks that

97

might exist after the compression is applied. While this is a generalization, master bus compression is used as a more noticeable sound-altering/enhancing effect, while master bus limiting is used more as a less audible "sonic safety control." Many of today's "master bus compressors" are actually really combination compressor/limiters, and offer both duties in a single plug-in.

EQ, compression, or both?

As with EQ, if your mix doesn't *need* compression or limiting on the master bus, then don't use them. If you find yourself using both, keep in mind that you can first apply EQ and then compression, or the other way around. As with individual parts, the order in which you apply them will give you different sonic results, so feel free to try them both ways and pick whichever order sounds best to you. As a general rule, I tend to apply EQ first and then compression, but either order is fine; let your ears be the judge.

Multi-band compression: combination EQ + compression in one step

Another type of master-bus processor that has become very popular in recent years is the multi-band compressor. As the name implies, these compressors work with multiple, but individually-controllable bands of something – namely, EQ – that are used as input to the compression process. So they're really a combination of EQ and compression in a single device. With these processors, the frequency spectrum is broken into three, four, five or more EQ bands, each with its own level control that feeds a compressor (in some varieties, all EQ bands actually feed a single compressor, but that's just design details). This means that you can compress just the bass and leave everything else alone, for example. Or you can add punch to the ever-important midrange frequencies where vocals, guitars and pianos mostly reside, while leaving the bottom and top end just as they are.

I'm a huge fan of multi-band compressors, and use them all the time in my mastering work. I find multi-band compressors to be incredibly flexible tools that enable you to "dial in" a great sound with just a single plug-in, rather than trying to approximate the same thing with several, separate EQ, compression and limiting plug-ins.

Here are some screenshots of some of my favorite multi-band compressors: MasterX3 and MD3 Multiband Dynamics from TC Electronic, UAD Precision Multiband from Universal Audio, and Steinberg's "stock" Multiband Compressor that comes with Cubase.

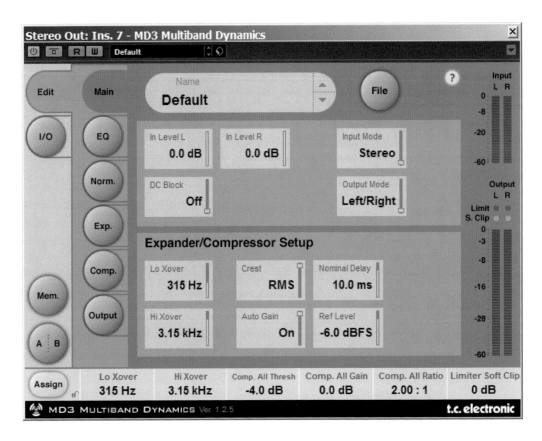

It's well worth spending the time getting to know one or more multi-band compressor plug-ins intimately. If you do, they can easily become your go-to tool for master bus processing. And of course, there's nothing stopping you from using them on individual tracks and groups as well, but as with anything, they can be over-used.

Set initial master bus other effects

You might be wondering when you would ever use other kinds of effects besides EQs, compressor/limiters, or finalizer/exciters on an entire mix. While less common, sometimes a very little bit of subtle time-based effects can do wonders for a mix. For example, if you've got a stereo mix that you recorded directly from the mixing board at a live gig, a little reverb (with a slight pre-delay) can put back in the ambience of the venue that's missing from the dry mix. You might also want to consider adding some creative processing to just one section of a multi-track mix for dramatic effect. A classic example of this technique is the bridge in the middle of the Doobie Brothers' mega-hit, "Listen To The Music," where the entire mix suddenly becomes awash in a flanging sound. Whenever I think of that section of the song, I can't imagine it without that signature effect. It's as integral to the song as the guitar licks or the vocals – it just *works*.

Another common effect used in master bus processing is a stereo widener. Here's a screenshot of a stereo widener that comes free with Cubase. It allows you to control the amount of "stereoization" that takes place.

Note that most DAWs don't have any send effect slots on the master bus, since it's considered to be the very last step for any audio processing. Depending on which DAW you use, in order to add a traditionally send-type effect (e.g., reverb or flange/chorus) to the master bus, you may need to create a group that you send all tracks to, add the effect on one of the group's send effect slots, and then send the group's output and the effect's output to the master bus. You could also use the effect as an insert effect (rather than a send effect) on the master bus itself, but keep in mind that if you do, you'll have less control over the input to the effect and will have to make any level adjustments on the effect itself.

Retroactively adjust individual tracks/groups based on master bus changes

Of course, adding EQ, compression, limiting, and possibly other effects to the master bus can potentially affect the balance between the different musical parts of the mix to the extent that they need to be slightly adjusted retroactively to bring them back in line. We're not talking about major surgery here; usually just some subtle raising or lowering of one or more parts' level will do the trick, so it shouldn't take very long. But as with every step so far, don't think you *have* to go back and tweak things just because you can. If it ain't broke, don't fix it!

Re-check/adjust master bus level

At this point, since you've added processing which could potentially change the output level of the master bus, make sure to double-check its volume and re-adjust as necessary to make sure it doesn't exceed 0 dB.

Export mix to stereo file(s)

And here we are, ready to export our masterpiece to one or more stereo files so that we can listen to it elsewhere. Since we're going to be using the resulting file(s) for critical, final listening, I recommend exporting to files that are as full-resolution as your target listening environment can handle. For example, if you mixed the song at 48 kHz, 32-bit float resolution and you're simply going to listen to it on a different set of monitors on another computer, then export the mix at 48 kHz, 32-bit float. If, on the other hand, you're going to burn an audio CD to listen to the mix in your car, then you're going to need to resample from 48 kHz to 44.1 kHz and optionally dither from 32-bit float to 16-bit. Fortunately, many DAWs today include automatic resampling and dithering as part of the mix exporting process, so it's really easy to spit out mixes at multiple resolutions from a single place. Worst case, you'll need to place resampling and/or dithering plug-ins on the master bus, or export a full-resolution mix and then use other software to prepare it for lower resolutions.

The following two screenshots show a dithering plug-in that uses the very-popular UV22HR dithering algorithm from Apogee. This plug-in comes free with Cubase. Note that the dithering plug-in is placed in the *very last* insert slot – after all other processing – because dithering is the very last change of any kind that should be done on the audio.

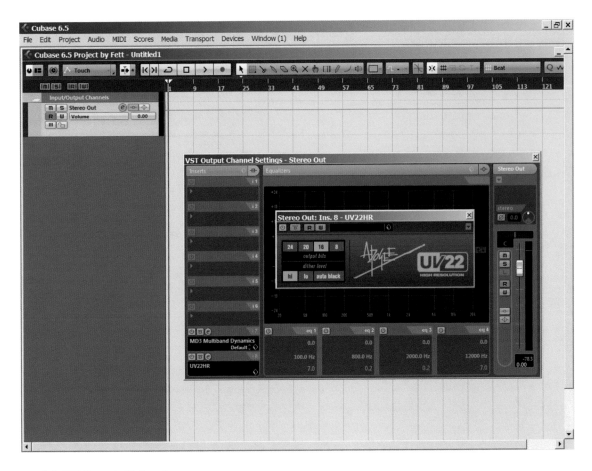

Avoid MP3s at this stage

Note that, at this stage, I don't recommend exporting your mix as an MP3 or similar data-compressed format, because the data-compression/encoding process, regardless of how high a resolution you use, will mangle the audio to such an extent that it will not faithfully represent all of the work you've just done for critical listening purposes. Sure, it will most certainly end up as an MP3 or similar format eventually, but for now, you want to be able to listen to your mix at as full resolution as possible. Fortunately, most software and hardware players today can play back full-resolution WAV and AIF files just as easily as MP3s or AACs, so there's no need to data-compress for playback.

If for some reason you're mixing a song for a client who is involved in listening at this stage of mixing, rather than sending a data-compressed version such as MP3 via e-mail to get around e-mail attachment file size limitations. I recommend one of the many free file-transfer services (e.g., YouSendit.com, Dropbox.com) to upload the file and send the client a link to it so they can download and listen on their end. It's a much better alternative to a crappy-sounding MP3 file, and will show all your hard work in its best light.

You may or may not want to export a "tracks-only" mix (with vocals muted) at this stage to listen to and double-check that the instrumental balance of the mix holds up. But remember: this is NOT the full mix, and vocals have a huge impact on how the mix sounds overall, so don't let the instrumental mix drive most of your decisions about mix changes. When it comes down to a choice, the vocal version rules!

Take a break, change headspace

The next step after master bus processing will be to listen to the exported mix and make some very minimal retroactive tweaks. But as with every other step in the process so far, I don't recommend making any retroactive changes before taking a break. You've had your head buried in master-bus processing for a while now, and you need to back up from that process and return to the 100-foot, end-listener level. If you come back and listen to the mix with your master bus changes applied after some ear-resting time away, I can almost guarantee you'll be more objective, and make fewer retroactive changes than if you apply them right at the tail end of adding master bus processing.

For this reason, I recommend that this break be measured in days rather than minutes or hours if you have that luxury. That's because at the final phase, you're going to be thinking more like a mastering engineer than as a producer or mixing engineer. If possible, I'd even recommend finishing Phase 5 mixes for all of the songs that are going to go together in a collection, and doing the Phase 6 pass through all of them as a group, but that's not always practical. The point here is to take a true break between Phase 5 and Phase 6 because, as you'll see, they really involve different processes and mindsets.

Phase 6: Multi-environment Listening and Final Tweaks

Listen to exported mix in different environments

It's a tried-and-true technique to listen to a mix on more than one set of speakers, and in multiple environments, before making final decisions and adjustments. If you're like most people, you'll spend most of your time mixing on the same set of monitor speakers. At this stage of the game, you want to verify that your mix will translate well across a variety of listener playback systems, so it's a great idea to listen to the mix through at least two *very different* sets of monitors at your mixing position if you have access to them. If you can't listen to two different sets in the same location, the next option is to listen on your mixing monitors, and then on your home stereo speakers or a boom box, then in your car, or any other environment that you're familiar with.

The car test

For me, besides my primary control room monitors, the "car test" is the most important step in the final listening phase of mixing (and mastering, for that matter). If you listen in your car, I learned the hard way that it's not enough to just sit in the car with the windows up and the music playing. It's critical that the car actually be on the road while you're listening. The road vibrations through the tires, wind passing over the vehicle, and the hum of the engine all play a huge part in what you're able to hear in a mix – especially dynamic range. Besides, most end listeners don't listen in their car when it's parked, so neither should you if you want to accurately adjust your mix for their listening environment.

No changes yet, just listen...

Note that for now, we don't make any changes to the mix. We're on the *listener's* side of the process now. As you listen, take notes on what you notice about the mix on the different speakers and in the different environments. Is it "boomy" on most speakers, or "thin?" In either case, chances are you're going to need some master bus EQ to compensate. Is the piano buried in two out of three sets of speakers? You're probably going to have to reach a compromise and bump up the piano part a little bit. And *compromise* is the name of the game here. No mix will sound perfect in every listening environment – it's just not possible because they vary so wildly. But what we can do is make the mix sound as good as it can *in as many different environments as possible*. If we do that, we've nailed it. During car tests, I use my smartphone or a small handheld recorder to dictate my thoughts in the moment as I drive. If I try to remember everything I'm hearing and write it down after I stop driving, I'm guaranteed to forget something.

You may notice that I haven't suggested listening on headphones or ear buds yet. In general, I don't recommend ever doing a mix primarily on headphones or ear buds, but *after* you've done the mix on monitor speakers, there's nothing wrong with using headphones and/or ear buds as one of the alternate listening environments, but always defer to speakers first. Why do I say that? In my several decades of mixing experience, more often than not, a mix that sounds really good on several sets of monitors will sound killer on headphones and ear buds, but it's almost never true the other way around. That's because the frequency response of most headphones and ear buds (as well as how our ears physically respond to them in such close proximity) is extremely skewed and doesn't even remotely reflect reality. Other than spot-checking for problems, I rarely ever pick up a set of headphones while mixing. The only slight variation on this rule is, if you absolutely know that the bulk of the end listeners will be listening to your mix on ear buds, then you might lean towards them a little more heavily – but still do the mix on speakers first.

Make final adjustments to individual tracks, groups and master bus

However many different environments you listen in, once you've written your notes or recorded your thoughts verbally, it's time to consolidate the information, look for patterns, and then make ONLY those changes that are necessary to fix any anomalies. If three out of four of your listening tests yielded a note about the mix being too bright, then you know you're going to have to tame some upper-mid to high EQ on the master bus. On occasion, you're going to have a note about something like the lead vocal being a little buried in the bridge, so you know you'll have to go back to the track/part level and make a tweak or two in the automation, but those things should be pretty rare at this stage, and this process should be fairly quick.

When is a mix "finished?"

Sometimes it can be tough to know when a mix is as good as it's going to get. I find that taking frequent breaks during the process helps to make everything go faster in the long run, and cut down on unnecessary, repetitive changes. Here are a few questions to ask yourself to help decide when it's time to declare your mix officially DONE:

1. Am I still serving the prime directive? Way back in the beginning of this book, we talked about the overriding goal of mixing: *to most effectively convey the message and the feeling of the song for the purpose at hand*. If you find

yourself making a bunch of twiddly little changes without really knowing why, or doing things that don't serve that driving purpose, then it's probably time to wrap it up.

2. Am I doing this for me, rather than for the song/client? Sometimes we get into a mode where we've been working on a mix for so long that we forget that our purpose is to *mix*, rather than to learn about, play with, or get overly-creative with our toys. At this point, we're focused inwardly – on ourselves – rather than outwardly on the song (and possibly, a client's song). This is the time to consider whether whatever time we're spending tweaking could be better spent on something else, and let the mix stand as-is.

3. Has my left brain kidnapped me? When we're trying to walk that fine line between the creative and the technical, we start out to make a change for musical purposes, and end up stuck in the middle of the change for totally technical reasons. Much of this is caused by all the visual feedback we get from mixing on computers nowadays: Hmmm, something about the slope of that cross-fade just doesn't *look* right (although it sounds just fine!)... Why do those two compressor presets sound exactly the same to me, even though they have totally unrelated names...? Hey, I can change the color scheme on a whole group of tracks in just one step with this combination of key presses...! You get the idea. At this point, it's time to step away from the geeky dark side and get back into musical mode.

4. What's the deadline? Sometimes having a fixed due date (especially from a paying client) is the best thing to keep us from overdoing things. If you're close to your deadline for the mix, you should take a step back and ask yourself what *minimum* tasks remain to get the mix sounding really good (if not perfect). I learned the hard way that making a few "just-one-more" changes at the 11th hour will almost invariably come back to bite me in the ass. Going back in to make five "quick" volume changes on a background rhythm guitar part can result in our inadvertently burning a mix with another part completely muted out because we didn't give ourselves time to go back and listen to the whole thing one more time. When the deadline is near, make only those changes that are absolutely necessary to fix true problems. Otherwise, leave it alone!

5. Is this déjà vu all over again? If you find yourself making changes that you're sure you've made before, or working on the same part or section over and over again, chances are you're too close to it and are beating it to death. This is the time to ask yourself, "am I actually *improving* the mix (rather than just tweaking for the sake of tweaking) or *fixing* a real problem with this change?" If the answer is no, it's time to let go.

6. Am I just being picky? One of the best qualities of a great recording engineer is extreme attention to detail. It means that mistakes will be caught early on in the process, no stone will be left unturned, and potential disasters will be avoided. But this anal-retentive quality also has a down side: sometimes we just don't know when to quit for our own good. While obsessiveness is a key trait for being a great engineer, being able to see the big picture at all times is a key trait for being a great producer. Great mixing lives smack at the intersection of these two traits. Will that seventh quarter-decibel adjustment in level on the left drum overhead track really make any difference in the musicality or feeling of the mix in the long run? Probably not. When we get to this point of repetitive, micro-detailed changes, it's time to get closer to the woo-woo side of ourselves and let our "inner producer" take charge and say, "enough is enough! Print it!"

Re-export final mix to stereo file(s)

Now that the mix is done, it's time to export it to a final set of stereo files. The reason I say files (plural) is that you have more than just "The Mix" to render. At a minimum, for vocal songs, you'll want to export both a "full" version with vocals and a "tracks" version with just the instruments. You might also want to export a hybrid version with instruments and background vocals, but no lead vocal. Even if you're absolutely sure (or the client tells you they're absolutely sure) you'll never need a mix without vocals, I can promise you, at some point in the future, you absolutely will! Rather than going through headaches at a later date to create those mixes (assuming you'll even have a compatible setup by then), export them *now*. It only takes some minor track muting and a few extra minutes. Trust me: you'll be glad you did. Here are just a few examples of why you (or your client) might want vocal and instrumental versions of mixes:

1. The "tracks" mix might be used for film or TV someday;
2. You might re-write the lyrics or melody and can re-sing it over the "tracks" mix and blend it into a new mix that uses only two tracks, instead of having to go back to Square One; or
3. You might find yourself needing to sing live over your tracks + background vocals mix at a huge award show.

There are plenty more examples than these, but you get the idea. You just never know, so save yourself future headaches (and possibly, missed opportunities) now.

Vocal and non-vocal mixes are just one set of mixes you might want to export. Here are a few other examples:

1. Mix with and without master bus processing applied (especially if the mix might be mastered);

2. Vocal-up and vocal-down (by a decibel or so) for mastering (your mastering engineer will love you for this!);
3. Bass-up and bass-down (by a decibel or so) for mastering (ditto on your mastering engineer);
4. Stand-alone "stems" (i.e., sub-mixes) of grouped musical parts of the song, e.g., drums, guitars, keys, bass, lead vocals, background vocals for mastering (your mastering engineer may hate you for this!) and/or potential "alt" mixes; or
5. If your DAW allows for it, both full-resolution WAV/AIF and encoded MP3/AAC, etc. formats (why do it in another step/program if you can get it done right here?).

Phase 7: Wrap-up and Housekeeping

Just like there's a Phase 1 to get the environment properly set up before we ever start mixing, there's also a final phase (albeit a short one) where we've got to do a little housekeeping to cover our butts.

After the mix is done: backups and archives

Once you've exported every conceivable version of the mix, it's time to do some "insurance" work. Assuming you've followed the methodology faithfully and made interim local backups at each step, now it's time to make a complete local backup of everything *on a physically separate drive* from your Projects drive, and preferably not even on the same computer.

Backup media options

Here are some options for media on which to store the backup:

- Hard drive (traditional spinning-platter version, or solid state drive)
- Thumb drive (typically USB)
- DVD-ROM or CD-ROM (if everything will fit)
- Smart media (SD, Flash, etc.)

Keep in mind that data safety is the main driver here, followed by convenience, and finally by speed of access. Hard drives (and the increasingly popular, no-moving-parts solid state drives) are the fastest, but they're potentially costly and do fail over time. DVD/CD-ROMs are super-inexpensive, fairly reliable over time, but slowest to write to. Most smart media (such as those used in cameras, cell phones, etc.) are small and portable, but potentially slow and pretty flimsy. Although they're fairly slow to write to, I happen to like thumb drives, because they're very portable, pretty ruggedly constructed, fairly inexpensive on a per-gigabyte basis, and extremely high-capacity for the size (32-, 64- and even 128-gigabyte thumb drives are commonplace now – that's a LOT of room for a lot of files!).

One for me, one for you...

If you're doing mixing for clients, I strongly encourage making two copies of all files on thumb drives, keeping one for you (only as a disaster backup) and giving the other to clients to take with them. At that point, you relinquish yourself from all potential liability should your own copy be damaged or destroyed. I can't stress enough how important it is to impress upon your clients that THEY need to make another safety copy of their thumb drive as soon as possible after leaving your studio. Just in case, I always keep my copy of their files until they tell me explicitly that they've made their safety copy. You can never, ever be too careful when it comes to this sort of thing. And, Heaven forbid, if they haven't made their own safety copy and something happens to their thumb drive, you can end up being a hero to them. Note that keeping your own copy of their files is strictly voluntary and out of the goodness of your heart – you're not obligated to do that if you have given them a copy. Do whatever feels right for your situation; I just tend to err on the side of paranoia. ☺

Remote backups

In addition to your own local safety copy and your client's copy, I strongly recommend making an additional, *remote* copy of all files. This can be either a physical copy that you store in a different geographical location than your studio, or a virtual copy stored in the "cloud" or other Internet-based service. Fortunately, there are more of these types of services arriving all the time, with prices plummeting in tandem. Just as with your physical copies, it's up to you to decide how long to keep remote copies after you've given the client theirs, but online storage is phenomenally cheap and doesn't take up any real estate in your studio.

Pie in the sky

If your project is such that you don't have in-person contact with your client, you can use one of the many Internet-based file-transfer services (YouSendIt.com, SendThisFile.com, Dropbox.com, etc.) to "send" the files to the client, enabling them to download and store them and make their safety copies at their location. These file transfer services are accessible from anywhere in the world, and many of them also offer online storage and backup, so you may be able to handle several housekeeping functions with a single vendor. Many of these services even offer a free subscription for basic file transfer of reasonably small amounts of data (e.g., 50 megabytes at a time). That might not be convenient for a multi-song music project with lots of multi-track files, but for DAW project files or a single song's multi-track files, it might be all you need.

Archival storage

So far, we've talked about making backup copies immediately after the project is finished. Over time, you might decide to copy backups of projects that you don't expect to work on in the foreseeable future to *archival* storage. The options for archival storage are basically the same as for backup storage; only the function is different. Many studio owners will put their local backup copies (for more immediate retrieval) on media like hard drives, and archive copies (for less time-critical retrieval) on thumb drives, or local backup copies on thumb drives and archive copies on the Web. You can use whatever works best for you, but you MUST have something in place, or you will be guaranteed to lose valuable, irreplaceable data at some point in the future. And that applies whether it's clients' data or your own life's work. There's absolutely no question that *every hard drive will fail at some point; it's only a question of when.* On a couple of occasions in the past when I've gotten lax with my backup and archiving routine – even for a few days – I've paid dearly in some fashion, whether paying thousands of dollars to have a hard drive reconstructed by a professional recovery facility, or (in the worst instance) having to tell a client he had to re-sing his lead vocals on a couple of songs – on my dime, of course. Ouch!

Celebrate!

WE. ARE. ACTUALLY. DONE! While you've enjoyed many moments during the mixing process, now you can truly relax, look back on your accomplishments, and give yourself props for a job well done. For me, finishing a mixing project brings with it great emotional release and a deep sense of satisfaction. That's why, after thirty-plus years, I still love doing it. I hope this book has helped you get closer to that same sense of achievement I feel, and even given you a few significant "ah-ha!" moments along the way. May life bring you many, many satisfying mixes, and remember that ultimately, *it's all about the music*!

Fett

15359423R00064

Made in the USA
Charleston, SC
30 October 2012